**2010 has been designated
The International Year of the Nurse by the
Nightingale Initiative of Global Health to Celebrate Nursing**

My heartfelt thanks go to Reverend Joyce Fisher Pierce and Unity Christ Church of Bon Air for the opportunity to learn and teach the Unity principles of abundant living to others. Much gratitude is also given to Mary Morrissey, my esteemed mentor and creator of the Prosperity Plus program. Many of the lessons applied to my life in this book came from principles learned through Mary's course and Stretton Smith's 4T Prosperity Program, both of which I have had the privilege to facilitate to willing students of life.

A portion of the proceeds from this book will be donated to nursing and health care scholarships at nursing schools and community colleges to assist in the education and training of individuals with a heartfelt passion to care for others.

CONTENTS

CONTENTS

CONTENTS

FOREWORD

by Hugh Gouldthorpe

The late, great Norman Vincent Peale, pastor of Marble Collegiate Church and author of *The Power of Positive Thinking*, once talked about the fact that we all have music inside us. That music manifests itself in terms of our attitude, caring for others, passion for learning, determination, willingness to go the extra mile, sincerity, compassion, and having a heart of gold. He went on to say, however, that so many people live and die with all of their music still within them. What a pity, waste, and a missed opportunity to achieve greatness and make a difference in this world.

This book is for those individuals who dream to be successful and prosperous and who want to make a difference in the lives of those they touch. It's not for the faint of heart, but for those who understand that the only limitations they have are those that they place upon themselves. Debbie Johnston is one who is committed to never letting a single note of music die within her. Her commitment and desire to excel creates a symphony second to none.

Debbie is the driving force behind the incredibly successful Care Advantage, Inc., where she oversees 12 satellite offices in Virginia employing over 3,000 health care professionals. She conducts her businesses in a most professional and caring manner. Debbie is a fierce competitor who refuses to tolerate mediocrity in others and the care her organization provides to her clients. She is a true giraffe in her industry, where she stands head and shoulders above the crowd.

Why has she been so successful? What are her secrets and what makes her so special? The answer is simple. It's her heart, which is giraffe-like in size. Giraffes have the biggest hearts in the animal kingdom, weighing 28 pounds and measuring two and one-half feet long. Compare this to the average human heart, which weighs less than a pound. Her big heart is the heartbeat of her successful organization and its phenomenal growth.

Debbie, like great entrepreneurs, has superior vision. Vision is simply where one wants to be in three months, six months, or five years from now. At the young age of 10, Debbie had a vision that revolved around creating the best life she possibly could. There is a verse in the Bible from Proverbs 29:18 which simply states, "Without a vision, the people perish." Debbie took that passage to heart, never looked back, and the results speak for themselves.

One of the greatest entrepreneurs of our time, or any time, was Sam Walton of Walmart. In his book *Made in America*, Chapter 17 is entitled "Running a Successful Company: Ten Rules that Worked for Me." Rule #10 is Swim Upstream. Debbie has adhered to that rule throughout her entire career. She has never been afraid to stick her neck out, to do it her way, even when others were critical and expressed doubt. She is always seeking the new, coloring outside the lines, and daring to be different.

I could write volumes about Debbie, her business success, and her passion for life. But you need to read this amazing story about a lady who refused to let the trials and tribulations of life deter her from reaching the goals she set and dreamt about. This heartwarming story will bring music to your ears.

INTRODUCTION

Every single second of every single day, someone, somewhere has an idea that could become a multi-million-dollar enterprise. The problem is, for every one of those ideas, there is someone, somewhere saying, "That won't work" or "That can't happen." Often, it's the voice inside the head of the very person proposing the idea. Too many times, that's all it takes—and another potentially great idea goes off to the wasteland where dreams can't come true.

I realize now the irony in the curious way I doodled hearts in the margins of my notes in nursing school. I find it astonishing that I am the owner of a wildly successful company that is all about heart. Our corporate office is a large pink box of a building with a red heart on the front, facing a major road. To say you can't miss it is an understatement. Sometimes destiny has a way of seeping through from your subconscious mind onto the very pages of your life.

This book is the true story of my idea to provide extended care for the many sick patients being released too soon from the hospital where I was the recovery room charge nurse. I had more than my share of people who thought I had lost my mind when I decided to give up my esteemed and well-paying position at the hospital to start over in a new field of nursing care. The naysayers came out of the woodwork, saying, "But you're in a big hospital—what about your benefits? You're at the top of the ladder—are you crazy?" The little voice I knew so well responded with its own doubt: "They might be right. Suppose this is not such a great idea after all?" Later, when the opportunity presented itself to actually start my own home health care company, I still questioned my abilities and balked in fear of following my heart. These feelings are not unusual, but it's what you do with them that matters.

That's why I am elated to be able to share with others how prosperous one's life can turn out when the courage to dismiss fearful thinking is found. Following through on one idea, despite the well-meaning voices of doom all around me, has made a tremendous difference in my life. Today, as the president and CEO/owner of three companies under the umbrella of Care

Advantage, Inc., my idea to care for patients in their homes has become the multi-million-dollar reality of my dreams.

I hope my story inspires someone, somewhere to find the determination from within to step forward and keep moving toward the reality of the dream they question.

CHAPTER ONE

LISTENING FROM INSIDE THE WOMB

Sometimes my business success amazes me to the point where I almost feel guilty. I was thinking about that on the way to an awards program not too long ago. As I cruised along in my little red Mercedes convertible, I felt blessed that I had been able to use a portion of my financial success to give back to people and causes that mattered to me. That day, I was en route to receive an award for community service. Upon my arrival and to my utter surprise, I found that I was the sole recipient of the award—the entire program was dedicated to me!

My father and I sat at the head table as many business leaders and community dignitaries watched a video of my colleagues, employees, and my family giving testimonials about my life. I could hardly believe that I had been chosen when there were so many other deserving people who could have been honored. Those feelings of unworthiness were familiar to me and can be traced directly back to my childhood.

I am living proof that the proverbial silver spoon does not have to be present at birth for things to turn out well. In fact, life didn't start out particularly grand for me at all. My self-determining negative thoughts began before I took my first breath of life. The feelings that formed words around me for nine months in utero were probably ones like "shame," "taboo," "embarrassment," and whispers of "We have to send you away." I may not actually remember hearing the words being spoken, but I know they left their stain on my inner spirit.

I was a love child, meaning I was conceived out of wedlock, but not necessarily out of love. "Love child" is a nice term for a bad situation. As was true in my case, my biological father would not be leaving his wife to marry my birth mother as she had thought. Instead, my mother was sent across the country to stay with her sister out of sight while I took shape in her body, but not in her world.

The first three years of my life were filled with ambivalence. My mother dropped in and out of my life like a distant relative. In the end, she could not overcome her demons to accept the responsibility of raising a child. Fortunately, her sister and brother-in-law loved me as their own child and wanted to adopt me. So my mother took their offer as her opportunity to walk away. I guess this could be seen, in reflection, as my first real break in life. Richard and Eunice Johnston were the most loving and devoted parents I could ever have hoped for. If it had been possible, I would have picked them out myself.

We moved from California to Virginia when I was three years old. My dad moved us in with his parents and became an electrician after leaving the Air Force. My beautiful, vivacious mom became an executive secretary for Lucky Strike, a local tobacco company. Happy memories of my childhood evolved from living on a farm and being surrounded by four younger sisters and a brother.

Wendy and I were born 11 months apart. We did everything together: catechism, learning to drive, and double-dating. Wendy was a model beauty. She had long legs and blond hair, and I felt so inferior to her. She'd cook, and I'd wash the dishes. There were moments when I felt just like Cinderella—before the ball. Mom made us go to charm school to learn how to walk properly and act like ladies. Wendy and I were inseparable for four years, until baby Susan showed up.

Susan was the beautiful tomboy. Dad called her his "boy named Sue." She loved fishing and horseback riding and always had such a happy disposition. To this day she is the most peaceful member of our family. She appreciates the small gifts and can thrill at something as simple as planting a flower.

Her contentment with her station in life brings her incredible serenity, and she is a joy to be around because of it.

Jill is my third sister, and I was six when she was born. I thought she was so adorable, and I pretended she was my own baby doll. Jill was always the quiet, introspective one in the family and still keeps a lot to herself. She has always been mature for her age and even ended up marrying Bob, one of her high school teachers. Jill is extremely loyal and would later take on a key role in my business life.

I think my parents thought they were done after Jill was born. But, on the way home from Williamsburg one day while we were all in the car, my mom sprung the surprise on my dad that she was pregnant again. He flipped out at hearing the news, exclaiming, "We already have four children!" But he got over it after the shock wore off. I still remember me, my dad, and Wendy sitting at home, waiting for the doctor's call about the delivery. When my dad answered the phone, the doctor asked him what he wanted, a girl or a boy? My dad said since he already had four girls, he was hoping for a boy, but as long as it was healthy, he said he didn't care. That's when the doctor told my dad to sit down. He told him that he got his wish—a boy like he wanted, but the doctor told my dad something else. He got another girl, too. Yep, my mom had twins.

Mike and Tammy popped onto the scene when I was nine years old, and life became interesting, to say the least. My mom needed help, and I was the oldest child. Anytime of the night, you could count on one twin to cry and wake the other one up. My mom and I sat rocking them all night, and my teachers yelled at me for being tired at school the next day. But having twins was a real joy. Everyone wanted to take care of them. We dressed them alike for as long as we could, until they grew up, and Tammy told everyone they weren't related. They always had a special bond—the internal twin instinct—that the rest of us did not have, but they were opposites in their personalities. Mike was quiet, smart, and all boy. He told everyone he wanted to be a tractor when he grew up. But instead, he became the most educated one in the family. Tammy was assertive, outgoing, friendly, and stubborn, but always loving. She was always more like mom than any of us and very street smart. Both Mike and Tammy would work in business with me, many years later.

Taking care of the horses and all the chores that went with farm life filled our time. But I adored my dad's adventurous spirit and the things we did as a family to feed that side of him. The family vacations more than balanced the work we had to do on the farm, and even though we were very poor, he always found the means for us to travel around the country to campgrounds. We had so much fun together, and I grew up in an extremely nurturing environment, loving my life and my family.

Somehow, though, in my preteen years, word leaked out that I had been adopted. Kids teased me mercilessly, telling me that my sisters weren't really my sisters. This made me feel that something was different or wrong with me. Negative self-worth would begin creeping into my consciousness and my otherwise happy life. To compensate, I became an overachiever. I went to church, joined 4-H, got good grades, and smiled my way to a spot on the high school cheerleading squad. I made every effort to present myself as the perfect child. My achievements made my parents very proud of me, and that approval became a standard bearer for my life going forward. But there would come a time in my life when I would not be satisfied living up to the standards that others set for me.

Our childhood teaches us to be approval seekers.

PLEASING OTHERS HAS ITS VALUES AND ITS PITFALLS

CHAPTER TWO

AN ACCURATE DIAGNOSIS

My dad began mentoring me as a young girl to become a nurse. I can vividly recall receiving my first toy nurse's kit as the seed was being planted. So even though I had always wanted to be a secretary like my beautiful mom, I followed my dad's advice and began vocational training in high school to become a nurse. My dad thought nursing was a secure career that would always enable me to take care of myself in any kind of economic environment. I was fortunate to have a smart dad; he was right.

After high school, I continued on to complete the LPN program and knew without a doubt that nursing was a calling for me. I was happy with my achievement, but my dad's vision for me was bigger than that. He could see the "RN" behind the

Johnston in my name. So even though I wasn't at all sure I could handle the advanced nursing program, my vocational teachers affirmed their belief in me, and off to nursing school I went.

Because the training was held in a hospital where the student nurses worked while they learned, the three-year tuition was reduced to $3,000—an amount my parents were able to scrape together. Excitement gave way to sadness the first day as I had to leave my younger siblings. My mom had packed the car full with all my belongings, making it painfully obvious that I was entering a new phase of my life, separate from my family. I knew it would never be the same. As the family car faded from sight in the distance, leading away from where I stood, I cried tears of great sadness. My maternal instincts had me wondering how my little sisters and brother were going to be without me there to help take care of them. I felt alone in the world for the very first time in my life.

I missed my family for a long time. But eventually, as I became comfortable with dorm life, nursing school opened up a whole new worldview for me. I was off the farm and out of the rural landscape with its close-knit community. I was living in town now, close to every convenience I could imagine. Finally, I exalted in the feeling of freedom and thought it was a great time to be on earth! But school was tough—military school tough!

The uniforms we had to wear everyday could stand up by themselves. To top it off, there must have been 100 buttons that had to be re-inserted into button holes after every cleaning. You would not want to wake up in the morning before class to find that someone had removed all your buttons! That was the type of practical joke nightmares were made of. Our director was a drill sergeant with every hair in place, and in her world, rules existed for good reason. Her purpose in life was to enforce those rules. Showing up late or without your buttons in place would guarantee that her wrath would await you. If your shoes were not polished, you would have the privilege of polishing the whole class's shoes.

I attended nursing school during the Vietnam War era, and though I thought it would be extremely honorable to become a United States service nurse at some point in my career, my years in nursing school would be the closest I would ever come to a military experience. The curriculum was extremely regimented, with a 25-hour course load in the first semester. There was no time for students to gradually ease into this new academic discipline, and the dropout rate was high. We went straight through this tough schedule for 33 months, with no summers off. Fortunately, there were many celebrations to motivate us and break up the monotony. Every six months, we would receive symbols of achievement, such as our nursing caps or a stripe to put on our uniforms to represent an accomplishment. My family would always be there to support me at these events, and that was reason enough for me to look forward to them.

My classmates rapidly became my new family. We ate, worked, played, and studied together. Everything we learned, we practiced *on* each other. We gave each other shots, and we performed bed-pan duty and patient bathing on our nursing partners. Let's just say it was a bonding relationship like no other I had ever experienced.

I quickly found out that nuns were not the only ones who sang together. Each nursing class was its own glee club, and a poor singing voice would not get you excused from the club. We sang on the bus to and from Virginia Commonwealth University, where we took our classes in the sciences. Every few months, whether we liked it or not, we dressed in our board-stiff uniforms and were bused to churches all over town, where invariably we could be heard singing the Florence Nightingale hymn in full throttle. The words that follow are ingrained upon my memory, but don't ask me to sing them again:

I solemnly pledge myself before God and presence of this assembly; to pass my life in purity and to practice my profession faithfully. I will abstain from whatever is deleterious and mischievous and will not take or knowingly administer any harmful drug. I will do all in my power to maintain and elevate the standard of my profession and will hold in confidence all personal matters committed to my keeping and family affairs coming to my knowledge in the practice of my calling. With loyalty will I endeavor to aid the physician in his work, and devote myself to the welfare of those committed to my care.

I learned the rewards of working hard and playing hard in nursing school. Practical patient care was where I excelled in the program; academically, I was never anything close to a Rhodes Scholar. Luckily, I had brilliant friends like Marie, who was blessed with a photographic memory and the patience to help me. I also became friends with our visiting residents from other countries. A student resident from Egypt often helped me make up rhymes to memorize difficult science terms.

The tests were excruciating, and we would all stay up half the night studying together for them. But we looked forward to celebrating afterward by going to local pubs, where we met up with our party friends from the University of Richmond. These were the crazy days of streaking and panty raids, and the UR boys were an interesting diversion for us. They also served as our dating pool. If any one of them was ever mean or disrespectful to a classmate, we would unite in retaliation. The offender might be met with a bucket of water from the third floor upon entering the dorm if his offense was a mild one. If we really wanted to make a point, we would set him up with a hot date at a phony address. While he searched in vain for a nonexistent "hottie" at an address he would never find, we watched, doubled over in stitches, from a nearby vehicle.

I doubt I will ever again be part of a group with the depth of camaraderie and emotional support as my nursing class. The school regimen was such a tough thing to go through, but experiencing it as a group with such a feeling of oneness, made it not only a bearable experience, but an unforgettable one. Eventually, 48 out of 60 of us graduated together. We must have left our mark—they even retired the wretched uniforms.

The pride I felt in accomplishing my first major achievement on my own filled my soul with joy and confidence. I just knew that I was on my way to bigger and better things. It also meant the world to me that I was able to make my parents proud, especially my dad, now that those RN initials were behind the family name. I felt good and ready to take on the world.

*Sometimes others see for us a path
we cannot see for ourselves.*

CONSIDER CAREFULLY THE OPINIONS OF PEOPLE YOU TRUST

CHAPTER THREE

LIFE THROUGH THE EYES OF A NURSE

While a student, I served three months in each nursing specialty. During that time, I experienced life from cradle to grave. Some of my earliest and worst memories occurred on the night shift in the preemie ward at the Medical College of Virginia while holding tiny lives that fit in the palms of my hands. I could see and feel them trying so hard to breathe and thrive, and though I wanted to will them to live, there were too many times that they didn't. Each time the last puff of breath left a frail little body, I had the responsibility of taking it through a long dark tunnel to a place where many little bodies of dead babies were kept. I felt like the angel of death carrying them home. In this solemn place and time when the whole world seemed to sleep but me, the silence was deafening.

My three-month assignment—which seemed more like a sentence—in the psychiatric ward of St. Elizabeth's Hospital was a lesson in contrasts. There was no peace, no quiet in that space for anyone—staff or patient. The inconsolable screaming and moaning of lost souls continuously filled the hot, stale air. Over time, it would inevitably have its effect on a caregiver's state of mind. My nursing partner and I began routinely diagnosing ourselves, each other, and everyone we knew. It was easy to see how even if you weren't certifiably insane, you could become so, over time, in a confined place where so many people were mentally ill.

My first psychiatric patient was a 23-year-old man named Joseph. He was interracial, and he was beautiful to the eye. But Joseph did not see himself that way. He was confused and unhappy. He told me one day, "I have never known who or what I am." Joseph wasn't crazy, yet, but he was a danger to himself. The patients weren't separated by the varying degrees of mental impairment. Every aspect of Joseph seemed sane, except his negative self-image, which had taken him to the top of a bridge where he had contemplated ending his young life. The mind is a fickle friend, and I couldn't help but wonder if Joseph would make it out of this place in time.

When my classmate and I left the psychiatric hospital after our period of learning was finally over, we drove away as though we were being chased by something evil that might reach out and drag us back. We knew in our hearts that what we were able to drive away from physically would not as easily be erased from our minds.

The real-world application of my training came quickly within the health care environment. It's why I say that many of the important lessons I learned about life and business I learned through the eyes of a nurse:

Lesson #1: The Art of Persuasion

If you are not able to develop the art of persuasion, you will have a difficult time being an effective nurse, parent, or leader of any substance. My days were spent convincing people to do things they did not want to do. This was leadership-building material, and it would help me later in life as president of my own company. But as a young nurse, I was persuading people to roll over so I could give them the shot they did not want in their backside.

Lesson #2: Integrity in Relationships

The importance of integrity in relationships loomed large when someone's health was on the line. If a patient did not trust you, it was hard to gain their cooperation in doing the things that needed to be done for their well-being. Nurses were the frontline peacemakers for the physicians, but that did not change the fact that when a doctor entered the nursing station, we were expected to stand and surrender our chair to him. If the nursing staff did not first succeed in delivering honest and compassionate care, the doctors were going to have an even tougher time performing their jobs. It didn't serve anyone for the doctors to be unhappy. In those days, doctors were treated like gods, and gods demanded to be happy.

Lesson #3: Overcoming Adversities

There is something to be said about working in an environment where all day long you are watching people overcome great adversities, many of them harder than anything you have ever had to deal with. It's only normal to start thinking how we let the smallest, pettiest things stop us from moving one step closer to our dream or even something as simple as just being happy everyday. Try comparing yourself to the woman who has her breasts removed one day and her whole self-image changes instantly; honestly, how do your problems compare to that? Think about the man who loses his mate of 60 years to cancer and has to move to a nursing home. Compared to those situations, many of us simply don't have problems that qualify as reasons to prevent us from doing anything.

A personal example of this truth occurred when my sister Wendy was 26 years old. The attending resident, saddled with the burden of delivering the bad news, could not even look at this beautiful, independent woman as he told her she had multiple sclerosis. Her future would be a slow demise to a wheelchair or a bedridden life of stolen dreams. In a nanosecond, her life was changed and nothing could be done about it.

Every day, fresh examples of major life-altering difficulties surfaced in the field of nursing, reminding me to appreciate a normal life. It also made me fearlessly aware that there were no obstacles too big for me to handle as long as I had my health.

Lesson # 4: A Level Playing Field

Health is the great equalizer. Money, age, background, material possessions, and everything else thought to be important before you get down on your health quickly loses its perceived value. Every individual becomes part of the family of humanity in an instant. Nothing you have or do makes you any different from anyone else. Health becomes the top priority when you don't have it, and everything else quickly becomes secondary. I saw this principle come to life many times, but none more poignant than a particular scenario that held a personal irony for me.

Chemistry was not on anyone's favorite class list in nursing school. To make things more difficult, the only chemistry professor at the school knew it. She relished the power she had over the nurses in the program, because she was well aware that in order for us to graduate, we had to pass her class. There was no way around it; we had to get by her.

She made her course so difficult that she was feared by all the nursing students, but that only seemed to feed her ego and put a smile on her face. Her answer to every question that she did not want to address was the same: "Because God made it that way." Eventually, the tables turned on that professor. Years later, when she fell and broke her hip, a twist of fate landed her in the hands of one of her nursing students—me! The pain she felt from her break was etched upon her face and reminded me of the dreaded days I spent with her at the front of the class. I can still hear the chalk clicking its way across the board as she wrote long scientific formulas for us to memorize. But on this day, she had no choice but to rely on me and my nursing skills to get her past her time of struggle. I did not let her see my inner satisfaction of being the one in charge this time, but I know she could not miss the irony of her predicament.

I saw her humbled greatly by her vulnerability as a patient. Her memory of my struggle in her class could not have made her feelings of insecurity and helplessness any easier to bear. In the end, she lived through her fall, just like I lived through her class. I can only hope that the nursing students who came along after she was my patient had an easier time in her classroom than I did.

Lesson #5: Faith in a Higher Power

The last lesson I will mention is perhaps the most important life lesson of all. I learned very quickly that there is a higher power in charge. It was the rule, rather than the exception, for the unexplainable to occur. Patients who had every reason to be expected to live would die, and people no one expected to die would live. I saw someone have a routine gallbladder operation and never wake up. Can you imagine a 10-year-old-boy getting hit by a train, have multiple surgeries and live? Then try to imagine that same little boy playing near his home and getting hit by a car—and *still* live! Times like that made it obvious that someone or something greater than us has a plan, and we are all part of that plan. That belief helped with the extremely difficult part of nursing for me—losing a patient. I learned that my only responsibility was to do everything I could do to the best of my ability.

Eventually, I accepted that controlling the outcome did not belong to me. But there were still cases that broke my heart, like the time I watched my patient, a 14-year-old-girl, receive her last rites in the emergency room. I can never forget the horror on her parents' faces. The closer you were to the patients, the harder it would be to lose them. So I decided the only way to guard my heart was to create more distance between myself and the pain of everyday loss. In order to do that, I chose to become a recovery room nurse, where my close interaction with patients would be minimized.

*What you **do** with knowledge is power.*

IT'S THE APPLICATION OF LEARNING THAT IS IMPORTANT

CHAPTER FOUR

THE ASSEMBLY LINE OF PATIENT CARE

I felt more like a people mover than a nurse in the 1980s, when insurance companies took medicine hostage. My days were filled with conversations like this: "Nurse Pearce, please help Mrs. James to her car. Her wheelchair and oxygen feed will be right in and don't forget her barf bag and her bed pan. Mr. James, all the instructions have been included for you here on these five pages of aftercare suggestions. Your wife will need constant care for the next three days to a week. Please see that she is not left alone." Then I would rush back to discharge the next patient, without time to adequately address the concern I could see on Mr. James' face.

During this time, patient diagnosis became the criteria used for insurance companies to pay hospitals, rather than length of patient stay in the facility, as it had been. Basically, hospitals got a huge pay cut and were paid a lump sum for a particular diagnosis, whether the patient stayed one day or one month. Therefore, hospitals began adjusting the length of patient stay according to the amount of money insurance companies were willing to pay them, rather than whether the patient was well enough to go home. Mothers who had stayed in the hospital for three days to a week after the birth of their first child were surprised to find out they were being released the day after their second child was born.

I saw people throwing up on the way out. It didn't matter if they were sick, they still had to go; otherwise, the business side of the hospital was losing money. The sooner they got another patient with another diagnosis, the faster their revenues would rise. Outpatient surgery became the norm, and people would be scheduled to come in for a procedure with no overnight stay. It felt just like the heart had been surgically removed from patient care. I found myself wondering what was happening to the patients who had been sent home before they were well enough to take care of themselves. Who was taking care of them?

I had been a charge nurse for five years, and now three departments had been placed under my supervision. My line of responsibility fell just short of director of nursing—the top position in the nursing order of hospital administration. I noticed the hospital was also using me to go out and market to new doctors. If the hospital wanted a new laser procedure available, I would be sent to recruit a desired doctor into bringing his practice and his equipment on board. It was a cost-effective way of increasing revenue by offering new services while minimizing expenses.

It eventually occurred to me that if the hospital could use me in a marketing role to expand their offerings, perhaps my paycheck should be expanding more than it was. I began to search the newspaper for ads about home health. Immediately, I found a new national home health company that was hiring in my area. They were looking for someone to call on potential clients with patients needing home health care. Ignoring the doomsayers who were sure I was at the top of my game in the medical field, I accepted the sales position.

My boss was co-owner of the franchise company. He introduced me to my position by giving me a training manual to read. I would soon realize that the manual would be the extent of my training. I could hear all the fear-based voices ringing loudly in my ears when my boss called me into the conference room early one morning and began pounding his ring repeatedly on the wooden table where I sat frozen across from him. I felt the fear in the pit of my stomach as he growled the words, "Now go sell!"

I had no idea of who to sell to and no idea of what to say. All I could do was cry, and that's what I did when I left the room.

I will never forget my first sales call. I wandered into a social worker's office and found relief in the kindest person I could have ever expected to meet. Her name was Judith Poole, and though I didn't see any wings on her back, I would know they were there before the day was over.

She was just the kind of grace I needed. Instead of trying to fake my way through a sales pitch to look and act professional, I decided to be as honest as possible. I told her who I was and who I represented. But I also told her I did not have any training to know how to answer any questions she might have. I just gave her my vision of what the company was set up to do and how we could help her clients.

That sales call taught me that honesty sows the seeds for the greatest rewards. When I got back to the office, I was floored beyond comprehension to find that the kind social worker had called the company and placed a $300,000 annual contract for patient care! My luck started the wheels of fortune spinning in my head. If I could do that on the first try without knowing what I was doing, what could I do when I did know more about how to present this new concept of home health care? That experience with success paved the way to expanded possibilities in my thinking.

The grass became greener after that day. I formed many new relationships with people who would become lifelong friends and allies in the home health care industry and would help me immeasurably in ways I had yet to imagine.

When I visited the hospital to see the friends I missed so badly and heard them moaning and complaining about their jobs, it was easy to remember why I left. The old memories tumbled back in like dark clouds on a day when a storm is brewing. It confirmed that I'd taken the correct path toward the future I wanted. I was moving forward while the others were content to be safe in the comfort of their familiar misery. They traded what they perceived to be risk for that which they knew well, even though they weren't happy where they were. They couldn't muster the courage to see the potential in the unknown. I, on the other hand, was destined to ignore the bird in the hand and go after the two, or three, I knew were in the bush.

Comfort zones are rest stops to nowhere.

A KNOWING HEART NEVER LEADS YOU ASTRAY

CHAPTER FIVE

A HEART TRANSPLANT

The only problem with the new job, besides the mean boss, was not always being certain that the company would deliver the service I had sold to a customer. That bothered me a great deal. It wasn't my company, but it was my integrity that people bought into when a sale was made. After one year, I decided it was time to put the heart back into hospital care. So with some success under my belt and a lot more knowledge and experience in the field, I now felt comfortable enough to take the home health care concept to a large hospital conglomerate.

Without any arm-twisting, I was able to paint for them the vision of profitability that I had experienced firsthand outside the hospital setting. I recommended that they create a new hospital division for home health care, over which I would be the administrator. Because my compensation had not kept pace with my expanded responsibilities as a hospital nurse, I negotiated a bonus based on my results. No one had probably ever asked a hospital for this consideration before; I guess I had developed a little moxie along the way. I learned that if you don't ask for what you want or feel you deserve, you are almost guaranteed not to get it at anyone else's suggestion.

The hospital was floored by the incredible success of its brand-new baby. My division of home health care showed a hefty profit at four months old. I sold home health care contracts, led others to do the same, and discharged patients to integrated care. We were putting compassionate care back into medicine by putting nurses back with the people who needed them. I traded in my Chevette for a BMW—life was beginning to be a much smoother ride for me as well. The home health division appeared to be a win-win decision for everyone involved.

Sometimes it is not possible to understand why good things don't last. One of those times was right around the corner. Everything was going well with the division, perhaps too well. In a surprising turn of events, the chief administrator of the hospital system decided to spin the home health division off on its own and sell it. The new owner of the division was, surprisingly, the hospital's chief administrator himself.

Many people were left scratching their heads on that move, and I was one of them. The sale had all the attributes of a conflict of interest. I now reported to this man—the new owner of my creation, and our operational styles did more than clash. He attempted to retract my bonus plan and affect the way I did business, which may have been something I could have swallowed if I hadn't been so successful before he took the reins away from me. I lasted a year before I headed straight to an attorney's office to discuss my legal rights to my bonus money.

Buddy Allen was the best attorney that I knew. Buddy looked at my predicament with a wider lens than the pinhole my anger had me looking through. He wanted me to jump ship and swim out on my own. Believing firmly that I had the knowledge and the experience to start my own health care company, Buddy was determined to have me see his vision. However, he was much farther along in his confidence of my entrepreneurial abilities than I was. He was relentless and would not give up the idea of a new home health company with me at the helm.

At one point, I was offered what I considered a giant deal to start a home health care arm for another hospital, but Buddy insisted on an ownership piece of the pie for me. When the hospital walked away from the negotiating table, I was furious at what I perceived Buddy had cost me with his demands. As I sat there stunned beyond belief, all I could think of was what I would do to him when our feet hit the sidewalk. I was afraid to believe in the future he saw for me. Instead of feeling bad about the loss of my opportunity, he insisted I develop a business plan.

He was incredibly persistent in his desire that I see what it would take for me to be the successful CEO of my own company. The more I resisted, the more he persisted. I finally had no choice but to peek through his viewfinder and try to see the world his mind had in store for me.

Most entrepreneurs are excited and ready to embrace creating a business plan, with the endless forecasts, projections, and analyses of numbers and minute details for action. I, however, was a trained nurse, and I detested everything about the process. The biggest part of me despised this man for making me go through it.

Once the plan was miraculously completed, Buddy put his money where his beliefs were and became a major investor in the venture and in me. Care Advantage, Inc. was born in 1988 as the result of my struggle with the hospital administrator. The old adage "When one door closes, another one opens" was actively at work in my life in a divinely ordained way, even though I had fought it tooth and nail. As I mentioned earlier, there is a higher power in charge, even when we fail to recognize it.

With a brand-new company to love and nurture, it was as though I had given birth to the real baby I'd always dreamed of having. In that respect, I became an extremely proud and somewhat overwhelmed new parent, and Buddy, my friend and attorney, was the surrogate dad who had borne the seed through his belief in me.

*Just because we can't see where we're going
doesn't mean we're not on the right road.*

BE OPEN TO RECEIVE
OPPORTUNITIES THAT SHOW UP

CHAPTER SIX

A PRESCRIPTION
FOR SUCCESS

I had never envisioned myself as an entrepreneur, but once I was on the path of business ownership, it felt as right as a hand sliding into a soft fitted leather glove for the very first time. Leadership roles had always come naturally to me, simply because I could relate to people and they felt comfortable following me. But sometimes, even when you are good at something, it takes a while to find the best application for your calling. Luckily, some people sped up the process for me. Buddy was one of those people; he realized where my leadership strengths could best be used before I recognized it myself. I guess I had to grow into the vision of my true potential as a business leader. I was a nurse, first and foremost.

Just as it had before, the home health care business boomed when I applied my experience and knowledge to it. But this time, it felt very empowering to know that what I built would be mine. It could not be sold out from under me after I took it on the road to success. The first person I called on for help was my sister Jill. I had hired Jill to handle the billing when I ran the home health division at the hospital, and she stepped right up to help me in my new adventure of business ownership. Jill and I, together with Kay, a staffing employee, got Care Advantage off the ground and running.

The name I decided to give my company was a mission statement in itself. The business plan was created around the desire to provide a caring advantage in patients' homes for private pay. We would pick up care where the hospital left off by assembling a large base of quality-oriented health care professionals who would be ready and waiting to handle every kind of patient and client need imaginable, from skilled nursing services for after hospital care to everyday personal assistance and companion care.

Whether there was a need for rehabilitation and recovery, grocery shopping, note-writing, or telephone reassurance, we would provide the advantage of having caring assistants and professionals available who were passionate and committed to serving the patient and the family in need. Our company mission would be reflected in our goal to provide the highest standards of professionalism in our business practices and in patient care while giving our staff a plethora of pleasant yet challenging work opportunities.

My excitement and personal satisfaction in starting a business cannot be overstated, and we worked night and day to get the business going in the right direction. But I had other motivation as well: Buddy had co-signed a large bank loan for me to start the company, and I had never owed anyone so much money in my life! Money may not be a motivator for most people, but my mountain of debt and the molehill of money I had to pay for it lit a fire in me! Where I came from, you did not owe those kinds of sums without concern.

When we were as young as nine or ten years old, my dad gave each of us children an allowance of 50 cents a week. We could spend it however we liked, but we had to keep a ledger, detailing how we used the money. Each week, without fail, I would spend half and save the other half, which sounds pretty responsible for my age. But each week, without fail, my dad would have to sit me down on payday, when I cried about not having my whole fifty cents from the previous week. He would gently explain to me that I couldn't spend money and still have it at the same time. I suppose that is where I learned my first lessons about fiscal responsibility.

Everyone was totally committed to the company's success, but I was the rainmaker. All bets were on me. While Jill, Kay, and Andrea—who also became part of our team early on—ran the office, I did everything else that needed to be done. I called out all the stops and re-visited everyone I had met in the health care industry to drive in new business to my company. The on-the-job training I was forced to master alone with the home health franchise was being put to good use when it mattered most. There was no need for tears or fears this time around. I knew what I was doing when my feet hit the ground. I knew who to call on and what to say to them. I had an air of confidence as I explained how my company could and would fulfill their patient needs. This time, I had no doubts that the job would be delivered as promised.

We placed ads and hired a field of skilled nurses who were excited to have more input into the type of work they would perform and flexibility over the hours they worked. Because a hospital setting offered a far more rigid work environment, we were able to add happy nurses to our staff everyday. To say we accomplished immediate and phenomenal growth is an understatement. In the first three months, we earned an astounding quarter million dollars in revenues! The dollar value of our success accurately indicated that we were meeting a huge need in nursing services not presently available in the health care marketplace. Every day it became more surprisingly apparent that I was, in essence, leading the home health and medical staffing fields and paving new roads to business in the health care industry.

It also became obvious to me how wading through the struggles of my past positions had prepared me for better things to come. Had things gone the way I thought I wanted them to go with my limited perspective at the time, I would likely still be working for someone else and making them rich. The challenges that appeared to be huge setbacks revealed themselves as divine order in progress.

I interpreted the selling off of the hospital division that I started and Buddy's negotiating demands with the new hospital as monstrous errors at the time. But those very obstacles put me on the path of business ownership and a much brighter future. It is not easy to accept present-moment challenges as stepping stones that will take you where you are meant to be, but life is lived a lot easier when you take this view. Of course, "Faith in things not seen" has never been an easy ideal to hold on to, especially when the going gets rough. I would be reminded of that many times in the days and years to come.

In a very short span of time, we had hired 150 employees and contracted a few thousand hours of in-home care a month. Thanks again to my previously challenging and self-serving employers, I learned everything I needed to know about how *not* to treat employees. From the very beginning, I envisioned my company as a family unit that would grow and prosper together.

If we worked hard, we would play hard, and everyone would be rewarded. I thrilled in creating monetary incentive bonuses and contests with prize trips to faraway locations, like the Bahamas, or nearby whitewater rafting adventures for jobs well done. I had as much fun giving as the recipients did receiving the rewards.

We would celebrate together at holiday gatherings and throw client appreciation parties twice a year as we grew the compassionate-care company with a big heart at the center of its reason for being. No matter how busy we got or how caught up in the administration of the business, at the end of every day we made a conscious effort to remember why our company existed. The answer was always the same: Compassionate care for the patients we served. We would remind ourselves that every patient was a mother, father, brother, or sister of someone who loved them. It was our job to take care of them as though they were a member of our own family, and in a sense they were. They were our number-one reason for being, the heart of Care Advantage, Inc.

Our reputation for compassionate care grew quickly and was so far-reaching that I received a surprising call one day from the family of a huge star of the golden-screen era. We'll just call her "Helen" for the sake of confidentiality. I ended up in the difficult position of finding nurses willing to live in New York to care for this woman. She was elderly and not the center of the movie universe anymore, so she was not the happiest or the easiest person to care for. But because her family heard about our level of commitment to patient care and believed we were the best option for their loved one, we extended our reach all the way up the East Coast to take care of Helen and honor the reputation that our company was building.

I vowed early on that I would never forget to appreciate the people who helped me grow my company. They would always be like family to me. I believed that if we took care of the patients, our clients, staff, and management, Care Advantage would become one of the biggest and most successful companies in the home health care industry. Perhaps Helen was our symbolic star of destiny, because in a very short time, Care Advantage was poised for success of dramatic proportions.

Challenges are teachers with
important lessons for another day.

THAT WHICH WE FEEL
WE MUST CONTROL,
CONTROLS US

CHAPTER SEVEN

NURSING A BROKEN HEART

I first met my husband-to-be at a party. He told me he was in real estate, and that was a good introduction, because I had a rule never to date doctors. I knew that they were at least as busy as I was, meaning married life would consist of passing glances between comings and goings. However, I would soon find out that the man I met at the party was not in real estate at all; he was indeed a doctor. I relented and broke my cardinal dating rule.

Wedded bliss came to me about two years before I started my business. I wasn't sure what I could have possibly done to be so lucky to find a man who rocked my world. I felt that God had blessed me with a handsome partner who loved me and wanted to share his life with me, and nothing could have made me happier. I openly adored this man as though he had actually hung the moon in the sky.

Since my husband-to-be loved to fish, we planned to have our small wedding on his beloved boat. With rose-colored glasses firmly planted on my nose, I certainly was not looking for any of the ill-fated omens that now seem curiously symbolic of things to come. Perhaps a small tug on my heartstrings should have been more evident when the boat, named Paramour, French for "other love," broke down right before the wedding.

The overcast day presented uncertainty right up until the ceremony began, when at last a small sliver of sunshine peeked through the clouds. We spoke our vows on a Tangier Island tour boat that rocked gently over a fluid foundation. While the water beneath us felt tranquil and steady at the moment, everyone present knew it could change without warning at any given time, much like the marriage we were entering into. But, of course, none of those thoughts reigned over our day, and when my new husband kissed his bride, the glow around my heart could have outshined the sun on its brightest day.

Once my business became successful, I showered my husband with lavish surprises that did not come from his own pocket. I had so much fun thinking of unique ways to make him happy. One time I hired a limo to pick him up at the office, and I whisked him off to a spontaneous weekend with me in the Bahamas. In my eyes, we were living the best life I could imagine.

When I reflect on the giant pedestal where I had dutifully placed my husband, I wonder if perhaps my career training on how to treat doctors had expressed itself in my marriage without my realizing it. When my husband was building his medical practice, I became the proud supporter on his arm, working the room at black-tie events, marketing him to everyone I knew. I was a walking, talking billboard for him. People called us the star couple of the local medical community, because we looked so happy and were blessed with successful, growing medical businesses. I could not have agreed more as I beamed with pride. But there were a few people who wondered if my owning a more financially successful business than my husband's medical practice might prove to be a dangerous blow to his ego at some point. I didn't believe it. We were partners and on the same team.

The only thing missing for me in the relationship was a child of my own. Even though my husband was twelve years older than me and had three lovely children from his first marriage whom I loved, we had both agreed early on that children were something we wanted together. That reality was not happening fast enough for me

After four years of marriage, something changed in the way my husband acted toward me. It was subtle at first, and I couldn't tell if the changes were related to other things going on at the time. I just knew that things were not the same as they had been. When I asked my husband if he still loved me, he laughed off my questions and denied any wrongdoing, as if I were delirious for bringing it up.

One day he informed me that he had changed his mind about starting a new family, and he scheduled a vasectomy. My dreams of being a mother passed before my eyes; I was devastated. This was a major commitment we had made to each other, and he knew how much I wanted children with him. This life-altering decision had been made for me, giving me absolutely no choice in the making of it. I would not discover a possible reason until many years later.

I suppose when my husband began to withdraw from me emotionally, my subconscious mind started to revisit the feelings of ambivalence that I experienced as a young child with a mother who did not seem to care about me. Except this time I understood the void of love behind the ambivalence, and my heart ached with the hurt I felt. Things went from bad to worse for me emotionally, and one of my sisters decided to get to the truth of the matter.

We made a plan, and I left for the weekend. By Sunday night, I had the explanation I had sought, but not the answer I wanted—an hour-long phone conversation between my husband and another woman. What I had not wanted to believe was true: He was having an affair. I made the heart-wrenching decision to get divorced, and I asked the man I thought I would be spending my life with to leave. I knew I would never trust him again. Trust is as fragile as Humpty Dumpty—once it is broken, you can't put it back together again.

It would take almost twenty years before I would believe I understood why my husband had changed his mind about starting a family with me. While I sat on the cold sterile edge of an examination table in my doctor's office awaiting the results of an annual test, I pretended to know about the existence of my ex-husband's college-aged son that the doctor spoke of in casual terms. Given his age, this child would have been conceived during our marriage. This could have been the child I ached to have; but of course, it wasn't. I was stunned as I held my breath and my shock at bay. Though I have no actual proof of paternity, I was told subsequently on a number of occasions that my husband had fathered a child with a nurse he worked with while we were married.

This news was in some ways worse than the violation of trust I had already suffered. Not only had I lost my marriage, but there was potentially a child born during that time period that should have been mine. To make matters even worse, I would soon find out that the nurse rumored to be the mother was someone I had befriended. When her own mother died, I had taken her books about loss and read them to her. After my divorce and the sale of the big house, destiny placed this woman and me in homes directly across the street from each other. I watched her son grow up, riding his bike and playing outside, without a clue that he was probably my ex-husband's child. I was good to them and even mentored her on some business projects. How could she look in my face and smile at me all those years? This is where the bar on forgiveness gets raised to an all-time high.

The heartbreak of deception had quickly morphed into a double betrayal, and my nearly healed emotional wound felt as though it had been ripped apart and sprayed with acid.

I cannot be sure when the foundation of our marriage went from tranquil to rocky. But I do know that I was one of the last people in our world willing to believe it would ever end like it did. It would take me many more years to realize that it was likely not a coincidence that I chose the man I did to marry. According to many psychologists, we look for a mate to fulfill what was missing from our childhood. Unfortunately, we end up choosing what we recognize, and therefore we pick someone who ultimately gives us the same behavior that caused us the pain we were trying to escape. What are the chances I would choose the type of man who would go outside his marriage and father a love child like myself? Obviously, I went looking for a man who would be emotionally available to me, yet chose someone who was not capable of it—just like my biological father. Until we recognize our childhood patterns, we will continue to re-create the unhealthy dramas we lived there. Thanks to the subconscious mind, this happens whether you wear rose-colored glasses or not.

*Make sure your choices represent
what it is you want for your life.*

IT'S NEVER TOO LATE
TO CREATE A HAPPY CHILDHOOD

CHAPTER EIGHT

POWERFUL MEDICINE

If ending my marriage took courage, then rising above the deep sadness that buried me in the aftermath was going to take more strength than I could imagine me having. I felt as if I had lost everything. Losing my husband was only part of it; I lost a family, too. I was no longer related to the mother-in-law I absolutely loved and admired. She was a wise mentor to me in so many ways. Besides my nieces and nephews, the only children I had to mother belonged to my husband, not to me. I was in the lowest place possible, emotionally. As a nurse, I knew I could not remain in this state and survive with my health. But I had no idea how to get out of the despair that overwhelmed me.

Fortunately, as I wandered lost through my splintered life, I was blessed to find a local Unity church with an upcoming class that was guaranteed to change my life. That was all I needed to hear to convince me it was worth a try. It has been said, "When the student is ready, the teacher appears." I was desperately ready, and I wasted no time signing up for the class that I prayed would save me from the pain I could not escape on my own.

The class was called the 4T Prosperity Program and was organized around the 12 steps of Alcoholics Anonymous, which many self-help programs use. The four T's in the class title stood for Tithing of Time, Talents and Treasures, and the purpose of the class was to increase abundance in all areas of our lives. The teacher of the class was a kind and soft-spoken minister named Lynette, and she would become a respected friend and mentor for me during that rough time of my life.

Every week I went to the class, listened to the tapes, read along in the workbook, and prayed for a miracle. For 12 weeks, I became immersed in a period of self-evaluation that required me to think about the thoughts I entertained on a daily basis. That was easy—my thoughts were very angry ones directed at the husband who had turned my happy life upside down. According to the material, it was those angry thoughts that were directing my life now.

Each week the lessons I learned would teach me that as long as I nursed my anger and resentment, nothing was going to change for me. In fact, I might even get more of the same! For things to change for the better, I would have to take responsibility for my life and my thoughts. In other words, to move forward, I had to forgive my husband. If I was truly able to forgive him, I would graduate with a feeling of empowerment and be able to leave behind my life as an unhappy and angry victim. That thought sounded very promising.

This class was years before the book and movie *The Secret* introduced the spiritual law of attraction to the world, but its principles were the same—you attract to yourself what you think about. The course would empower me in ways I would never have expected. By the end of the class, I learned to forgive everyone I held resentment toward, and in letting go of the past, I opted for the promise of a brighter future.

I also learned about giving back according to the universal law of abundance called tithing. Tithing is the joyful giving of a full 10 percent of everything received monetarily to the source that feeds us spiritually. It seems a lot of people have trouble with the tithing part of the program. I had a memory ingrained in me from childhood that made adopting the principle a no-brainer for me. As a little girl, I lived near a grocery store called Ukrop's, named after the family that owned it. The chain of stores had been run by the family for generations. The stores were well-known locally for their cleanliness, high-quality food products, and excellent customer service. But the family was known for something else as well: They believed in giving back to their church and their community. They tithed their time, talents, and treasures in a hugely magnanimous way—they did not give 10 percent; they gave 20 percent, and they were extremely successful.

I learned all about the family and the principles they lived when I took a Bible school class as a young girl at the church they supported and attended in my community. I decided I was going to be just like them when I grew up. So when I heard the 4T spiritual principles as an adult, it was easy for me to embrace tithing in my business and personal life. Immediately I began stroking checks for 10 percent of whatever inflow of cash I received, the moment I received it. I could not believe how much fun it was for me to give that money away. I actually looked forward to getting, so I could give a portion away! Putting this principle into action caused a cataclysmic shift in my attitude and in my life. I saw my prosperity grow exponentially with my commitment to giving back.

My mom was the biggest cheerleader in my life. She praised my spirit of giving and told me over and over that I had a lot because I gave a lot. It has been 16 years since I adopted tithing as a guiding force in my life. During this time, I've gone from knocking on doors and begging people to pay me so I could make payroll to sitting on top of a multi-million-dollar company and living a life of abundance beyond anything I could have imagined. Giving in gratitude and without doubt has brought me enormous blessings. It has also let me know that I will always have more than I need, if not everything I want, and more than enough to share with the people and causes I care about.

The 4T course did exactly what it said it would do—it changed my life and the way I looked at life. In fact, it was so influential to my way of thinking that years later I became a teacher of the 4T prosperity principles. This gave me the chance to give back to others the hope and joy for living that was given to me. I saw sad faces coming into the class light up and leave happy. I saw hairstyles and clothing styles change during the course of the class. It was amazing to see and hear the personal growth in the students who took my class, and it always reminded me of how the class changed me. The lesson of forgiveness helped me stop needing to win or be right. I learned to let other people win, or at least to let them think they were winning.

Twelve years and hundreds of successful students later, I can heartily attest to the mind-expanding principles of the 4T Prosperity Program. I can also honestly say that the course was the miracle I sought to help me through one of the toughest times in my life. But it was more than that. It prepared my mind and my spirit for the abundance that would pour out like a blessing on me in the days and years to come.

If you are experiencing lack,
you are choosing lack.

"WHAT YOU THINK ABOUT, YOU BRING ABOUT"

–Stretton Smith,
founder of the 4T Prosperity Program

CHAPTER NINE

AN AMAZING
RECOVERY

Now that I had gotten my emotions in check and put myself back on course, I began to zoom in on Care Advantage, Inc. with a laser-beam mentality. As much as I loved my company, it never took precedence over the importance of my marriage. Once the relationship was over, nothing held more significance for me. I became dogged and determined to have my company replace the real baby I would never give birth to. I not only wanted it to grow strong and healthy, I wanted it to leap tall buildings at a single bound. I suppose it was possible that a little human resentment had slipped through to my subconscious mind and taken up residence in my soul; I could allow it to propel me forward or sink me lower.

Fortunately, another benefit of the 4T program is that you begin attracting people who can help you. A man I met through the program had a profound effect on how I handled the recovery phase of my divorce. He simply said that success is always the best revenge. He probably has no idea to this day how much that statement influenced my actions. He encouraged me not to be ugly or to entertain thoughts of getting even. The key to success was to change my motivation to becoming as successful as possible. I converted the negative energy of resentment into a powerfully positive drive that sent my company soaring into the outer limits of success. As I applied the power of intention with single-minded attention to the business of running my company, it would not be long before my wheelbarrow of lemons would become barrels of luscious, sweet lemonade—almost more than the storehouse could hold!

Care Advantage entered a period of expansion that changed the face of the company forever, and the business world stood up and took notice for the first time. We launched our first satellite office in Colonial Heights, Virginia, in 1991 for two simple reasons: The demand was there, and I loved the idea of my company becoming a chain. I tried the cookie-cutter approach to expansion, but operating in fifth gear like we did in Richmond did not work well in the small community of Colonial Heights. For the business to build the trust necessary to be successful there, we had to become entrenched within the community. It would take more time than we had originally thought.

The following year it was as though Care Advantage had suddenly lost its cloak of invisibility. The company was recognized as one of Richmond's Rising 25 Companies for the very first time. In 1993, the nurse in me who had not wanted to make a business plan was the first woman ever to be named Entrepreneur of Richmond.

In 1995, a tornado blew through the town of Colonial Heights and our office was directly in its path. I was in my Richmond office that day, engrossed in my work on the computer, when Andrea and my sister Jill came in repeatedly to tell me about the weather conditions in Colonial Heights. Tornadoes are just not big events in Virginia, so I did not grasp the severity of the situation until they came in with the news that the roof had been ripped off the Walmart store. Our Colonial Heights office, manned with four administrative employees, was directly across the street from that store! Now they had my full attention. With no cell phones or news reports to check on our office and staff, I could not get there fast enough, though my mind was already racing in their direction. I took off by car and drove as far as the Chesterfield County Airport, when I had an idea. I stopped at the airport, ran in, and rented a helicopter to fly me in to Colonial Heights.

When we landed in the parking lot of our office building, and I popped out, hundreds of National Guardsmen swarmed the helicopter and wanted to know who I was and what I was doing! The whole glass front of our office building was shattered and part of the roof had caved in. Tammy, one of my associates in the office, had lived in Kansas before and had recognized the sound of the tornado when it took the roof off the Walmart store. She immediately directed the handful of employees to the back room, where they took cover under furniture and, thankfully, all made it out safely. However, had the tornado hit 30 minutes earlier, when at least 50 field employees would have been in the office to pick up their payroll checks, we would very likely not have been so fortunate. It was a very frightening experience for the employees who were there that day, so I made sure they received psychological counseling to help them with the aftershock of our surprising Virginia tornado.

There was a lot of media attention surrounding this story. The helicopter idea seemed to create good headlines. In fact, when I was the first woman to receive the Ernst and Young 1996 Virginia Entrepreneur of the Year award, I was told that my quick action in renting the helicopter demonstrated a remarkable care-giving spirit toward my employees, and that had been the deciding factor in selecting me for the honor.

The awards kept coming after that, but I never stopped feeling like a child on Christmas morning when I received one.

I was always surprised to be picked. Caring for others has always been second nature to me as a nurse, and being honored for doing what I loved was an unexpected perk. However, the awards were confirmation for me and my associates that Care Advantage was on the rise as a well-run compassionate care company, and our efforts were achieving results consistently worthy of recognition in the business world. That knowledge in itself was rewarding.

Watching our competition closely, I became convinced that we were losing a hefty piece of the market share of supplemental staffing to our competitors. But no matter what I said, my marketing staff would concentrate only on the private duty piece of the pie. I could turn somersaults in seminars trying to get them to include staff relief services to medical practices in their focus, but they held on to their old ways of doing business like old dogs with their treasured bones. In 1998, I gave up cajoling them and forced the issue by creating a separate division called Nurse Advantage, with supplemental staffing as its sole function. Through Nurse Advantage, we began offering professional staff relief for hospitals, nursing homes, correctional facilities, retirement clinics, and other medical practices with personnel needs.

Like my employees, many people thought that supplemental staffing would never catch on, but I based my decision on my instincts rather than on the opinions of others. In a few short years, the Nurse Advantage division grew to become a multi-million-dollar business on its own, and the profit margins from this division were a key source for growth in Care Advantage's revenues during the first five years after its startup. As usual, focus and good instincts rarely lead you in the wrong direction.

A second new division, called All About Care, was formed in 2003 to address the short-term needs of Medicare patients. Skilled care for acute needs, such as physical and occupational therapy to speed recovery after surgery or an accident, was an area that we were not adequately set up to address. It's a difficult area to administer because of the many rules and regulations that can cause either a patient to be without care or the provider of patient services to go without payment. But as we found ourselves having to turn Medicare patients away, we were potentially losing patients to competitors who offered a full array of services for both short-term and long-term care patients. So we decided to set up a separate division to handle the administration of this area of need.

Even though this is still a complicated area to manage and a balancing act for profitability, especially in recessionary times, we have remained committed to providing this service. The future will likely hold many short-term needs for active baby boomers on the mend. Sometimes you have to gamble through the lean times to position your company for times of surplus.

Once again I found myself at a point of realization in my journey, where unexpected and undesired challenges—this time in the form of a broken marriage—catapulted me to higher levels of success. My company literally became a powerhouse when I thought I was at my weakest and most vulnerable. It was becoming easier all the time to see that worry is a wasteful activity.

I will be forever grateful to my amazing staff members who rallied behind me and Care Advantage during that rocky time in my life. They worked hard, stayed late, and encouraged me to continue growing my company. Among those core employees were two of my sisters, whom I love dearly, but all of the employees were like family to me. As Care Advantage celebrates 20-plus years in business, many of those employees are still the heart and soul of my company.

Today Care Advantage and its subsidiaries employ 3,000 people with the continued mission of providing others with compassionate care. It may be an old cliché, but it feels extremely good to say, "We've come a long way, baby!" Care Advantage may not have been the baby I had in mind, but I couldn't be more proud to call her my own.

It's amazing what a little fire in the belly and applied focus can do.

A LASER BEAM ZEROES IN; A FLOODLIGHT SPREADS ITS LIGHT TOO THIN

CHAPTER TEN

A DOUBLE DOSE
OF PAIN

With my company growing by leaps and bounds, just the way I envisioned it, I felt instinctively that the time had come for me to fly solo. Though it was difficult to even think of ending my business partnership with my attorney and close friend, Buddy Allen, I knew it was something I had to do. There was no question that Buddy had been instrumental in forming Care Advantage. His supporting role had been invaluable to me in the beginning like no other.

Buddy had given me a crash course in business management, which I would need to run my company effectively. He helped us find our first office, and he came in to hold monthly staff meetings with his commanding presence. When more money was needed to invest in the company, he secured the loans. But from day one,

Care Advantage was set up to be my firm with only a consulting interest in it for my partner. I shouldered the responsibility for keeping the doors open and handling the day-to-day headaches of creating consistent and sustainable momentum for the company. It was my job to drive home the business; I knew the industry, had the contacts, and secured the workload.

Now that I was single and on my own again, my financial future took on a new level of importance. My company would be the source for my lifestyle going forward, so protecting my interest in it was a huge priority for me. I had been fortunate enough to get my husband to sign a handwritten agreement before the divorce settlement that prevented either of us from having a stake in the professional business of the other. That would prove to be a very wise move.

As the number of employees and revenues continued to grow, our expenses soared and our operating cash flow tightened. When I started looking for financial leaks on the balance sheet, I found the payment to Buddy, my now-silent partner, to be a leak of huge proportion. I knew it was time for me to plug that leak by having sole ownership over the company that I led from the trenches and invested my life in every day. I poured my heart into my company, and I wanted to know I would always be in control of it, so I began talking to Buddy about buying him out. Unfortunately, he had no interest in selling his position.

Instead of us working it out together, we muddied the waters and distanced ourselves from each other with business brokers, bankers, and accountants. The brokers came up with what I felt to be an extremely high valuation—one I had no idea of how I could pay. I absolutely hated disappointing this man; Buddy had given me the incredible gift of believing in me when no one else did. He pushed me up when I did not believe in myself. Not only was his mentorship essential in getting the company started, but his friendship had been a grounding factor in my life for a very long time. But if Care Advantage was to be my future, I could not afford to have any concerns about ownership or profitability. I had already come out on the short end of enough business deals to know better than to leave this thread dangling for someone else to tie up.

As hard as it was, my decision was made. In a final negotiating meeting with Buddy, we assembled a whole host of professionals to broker the deal. As one would expect, Buddy's business broker put a higher valuation on the company than mine. With all the suits throwing their opinions around, increasing the pressure for me to sacrifice my position, I blew like the cap off a radiator with no antifreeze to cool the engine. I was done. I stood up and, in a bold move, told every professional in the room to leave. I must have made the impression I intended, because they all stood up and filed out wordlessly, one by one.

Through the tears that flowed to cool my temper, I told my partner that I would not pay what his broker suggested, and I gave him a figure that I would pay. It was not a small sum; I would have to run my business exceptionally well to be able to afford it. I wish I could say the buyout was a great experience for both of us. Unfortunately, it dampened a friendship that meant the world to me.

After about a year went by, I picked up the phone one day and called Buddy. I opened my heart to him and told him how much it bothered me to have this cloud hanging over our friendship. I wondered if he might consider taking me on his books as a corporate client. Thankfully, he agreed. Buddy Allen is still my attorney to this day, and it is always his advice that I turn to for protection in any important decision affecting my life. He is also the first person I recognize whenever I find myself accepting an award for Care Advantage. I have found success to be far more rewarding when I am able to acknowledge with gratitude and generosity those who helped me get where I am.

There are times when you have to lose a battle to win the war.

IN ALMOST EVERYTHING THAT MATTERS, TIMING IS EVERYTHING

CHAPTER ELEVEN

A CAREGIVER'S SPIRIT

One of the best things about growing a financially successful company is having the ability to give to others. I learned to adopt a caregiver's spirit early on from my grandma, Belva, in whose loving care I stayed while my parents worked. She was one of the most positive voices in my life. My earliest memory of her is helping me learn to tie my shoes by the story lesson of *The Little Engine That Could.* I can still hear us singing, "I think I can; I think I can." She made me the best peanut butter and jelly sandwiches in the world, and they remain my comfort food to this day.

Besides having a huge amount of patience, Grandma had enough energy to light up Times Square. For 10 years, she worked the night shift at a nursing home, and then came home to take care of my aunt's children so she could go to work. My grandma had the rare ability to love unconditionally and never raised her voice to anyone. I knew that even on my worst day, she still loved me. Grandma was also a devoted Jehovah's Witness and often took my sister Wendy and me to witness with her. She gave of herself fully in all areas of her life and was still taking care of her grandchildren's children when she was in her nineties.

I have often felt that God gave me the ability to make money, so I can give to my heart's content. At this stage of the game, I can't imagine *not* giving; it is such a joyous experience. I find it no coincidence that I started a company made up primarily of women, many of whom have been in unhappy marriages and miserable with low self-esteem. I saw many of them regain their confidence and self-worth through their responsibilities at work. It didn't take me long after my own divorce to see that my company was the place where the more I invested in it, the more benefits I got back, and the better I felt about myself. Once I recognized this, I wanted to provide this opportunity for the women who worked for me. I set out to dream up as many ways for them to win as I could think of. I offered them prizes for reaching goals—minks, trips, money, spa days, gifts, and awards. I also created incentive bonuses and career advancement programs.

One of my most ingenious ideas was the Heart Prize Program. It worked very much like the S&H Green Stamps program that my mom loved so much when I was young. She would be awarded Green Stamps for product purchases at participating stores, and when she had enough stamps to fill her book up, she would rush to redeem it for the prize she had chosen. The Heart Prize Program was built around the idea of caregiving. When employees performed according to the program incentives, they would receive pink hearts to fill their books for prizes. It was a big hit, and I received the coveted Working Women's Entrepreneurial Excellence Awards in 2000 and 2001, largely because of the Heart Prize Program and other incentives I created.

Incentives work to make people happy for a while. Unfortunately, there is a downside to relying solely on work to nurture you rather than a relationship or a happy home life. While we drown our sorrows in our work or give all of ourselves to our career, we are missing out on the greatest human experience of all—love. When women or men want to stay late and get to work early to escape their unhappiness at home, it works out well for Care Advantage, but the individuals sacrifice the balance between work and play that is so necessary for a fulfilling life. I have never had a dying patient tell me they wish they had worked harder or earned more money; I have had many say they wish they would have or could have loved more.

Caregiving comes naturally to a nurse, and Care Advantage offered me so many ways to satisfy the need I have to show caring. In the beginning, I was very involved with private duty patient care. There were so many special patients who became family to me and my staff.

Once I took care of two sisters, Estelle and Eula. Independent living was very important to them, so my mission was to do what needed to be done to enable them to stay in their home. They called on me for everything they needed. If they needed a roofer, I found them one. When it was time to put up a Christmas tree, I went out and got them one. I brought them their groceries and made sure they were able to have their mint juleps in the afternoon, like the true Southern ladies they were.

Estelle and Eula were brilliant at 80-something years old, and Estelle had her master's degree. It's amazing what you can learn from the elderly. These two were wise beyond their years. When Estelle died, I did my best to keep Eula in her home, living independently. Both women were adamant about never wanting to go to a nursing home, but after her sister died, Eula became disoriented and could not stay alone. I found a nursing home for her, but she died two days before she was supposed to move. It was a relief not to have to watch her go down a path she was so opposed to. She was family to me. It was not rare for our patients to become our family. Sometimes, we are the only family they have available to them.

Trixie was in her eighties when she was robbed after being awakened at night with a knife at her throat. There was a foot of snow on the ground at the time. Her son was a lobbyist living in New York, and he saw an article on Care Advantage. He was busy with his life and career and wanted someone to care for his mother, especially now that she was afraid. We literally became her family. We moved her into a retirement home and took her to psychological counseling. If Trixie needed anything done, we did it. There was no one else for her to call on. We addressed her Christmas cards, did her shopping, and put up her Christmas tree—just like family would do. She was a patient in our care for 10 years, until the day she died.

Through the years Care Advantage has had the privilege to donate over $500,000 to local charities in the communities in which we operate. I feel it is important to be good stewards of your money and your world. As it says in the Bible, "To whom much is given, much is required." I believe in that principle and live it to the best of my ability every day. Supporting the work of non-profit organizations is a great way to see your money make a difference, and there is a non-profit for every cause you can think of. They have their fingers on the pulse of what needs to be done in the world.

Early on I was inspired to support one of my favorite non-profits by a seven-year-old little girl from West Virginia; she was one of my first patients in pediatrics. She drew a beautiful picture of her family; everyone looked perfect in the drawing, except for herself. She had a cleft palate and she saw herself as very ugly. I can never forget the pain I could feel in her heart. I became a joyful supporter of Smile Train—what could be more joyful than to give a kid a smile? This year on my birthday, I asked my chief operations officer to pass the word that I would prefer everyone donate to Smile Train instead of buying me gifts. I truly needed nothing, and one smile for one more child would be a priceless gift for both of us. Getting birthday wishes by e-mail with a notice of a donation to Smile Train gave me big smiles, too!

Nursing was my dad's idea for me. He often asks me how I have accomplished so much. I think he gets a lot of the credit for helping put me on the right track to a fulfilling career in which I could express myself in amazing ways. I am filled with a grateful heart that my parents loved me and supported me in my dreams. Nursing is a wonderful career, one in which you can be anything and everything you want to be. You can go to a Third World country, travel the world as a medical crew member for a cruise ship, or review charts from behind a desk.

Helen is an example of one of the greatest nurses on earth. She started out as a military nurse and later worked a lot of hours for me at Care Advantage. Wherever we sent her, she would get rave reviews and people always wanted us to send Helen back. One day Helen developed a type of meningitis and eventually lost all four of her limbs. But there was still meaningful work for her in the nursing field—she reviews charts. Helen is now an even greater role model and inspiration for the field of nursing and the human spirit. She is also a terrific example of the many applications of caring that exist in the field, and she demonstrates my dad's wisdom about the economic advantages of nursing. I feel proud to have two of my nieces follow in my footsteps.

Other careers may pay just as much money as nursing, but many require more education and offer less opportunity. You can become a nurse and change the world—one patient or one chart at a time. That is why I decided to commit part of my earnings to develop the field. Care Advantage has committed to donate a quarter of a million dollars to endow a nursing scholarship fund through J. Sargeant Reynolds Community College in Richmond, Virginia. I am honored to gift humanity with more caring nurses through this scholarship program. The world can never have enough nurses.

Caring is the essence of nursing.

WHEN YOU'RE A NURSE, YOU KNOW THAT EVERYDAY YOU WILL TOUCH A LIFE OR A LIFE WILL TOUCH YOURS

–Author unknown

CHAPTER TWELVE

DEALING WITH DEATH

One might think that being a nurse would toughen you up to the experience of loss after so many run-ins with death and dying. That may be the case for some, but it did not work that way for me. Every loss was painful. So when I began to experience the personal pain of losing those I loved, I was never prepared. I believe with all my heart that people have a knowing about their impending death. I have seen this truth displayed time and time again. Consider the different responses I saw from women who faced a potential issue with their breast cancer screening. Those who were able to voice their hope that they didn't have the disease would most often end up not having it. It was the quiet, reflective ones who kept their thoughts to themselves who knew. They were afraid to have the words tumble out over their tongues and into their world, because innately they knew that something was wrong, and they did not want to confront the reality openly, as if denying it would make it disappear. There is wisdom in the words—what we resist persists.

My brother-in-law Bob was one of the smartest people I had ever known. He helped me with my company's bookkeeping. Over a two-week period in 1991, Bob suddenly began losing a lot of weight. At first, he claimed he was dieting. Then back pain rendered him sleepless. After he began throwing up, he relented and went to a doctor. He called his wife—my sister Jill—and said, "They are sending me to the hospital. I am probably going to die." There were no diagnoses at this point. His health issue was thought to be gallstones.

When the diagnosis came on November 5, 1991, it was as bad as Bob had thought it would be. The lymphoma that was suspected became pancreatic cancer through diagnostic tests, with a 1percent chance of survival. Bob lost a pound a day for 90 days. I saw him move in stages from a happy, vibrant man to one who began to push the activities and people he loved aside in preparation for his final transformation. Hopelessness, anger, and hurt accompanied the recognition that he was going to be leaving the people he loved much sooner than he had ever anticipated. He quit his job and the game of golf he loved. He was saying goodbye to his life, bits and pieces at a time.

Sometimes people mistake the dying person's actions as anger directed toward them, when in actuality, it is just the necessary acceptance taking place. Nevertheless, the inward pull has a devastating effect on those left behind. I watched my sister age 10 years in those 90 days.

My nursing classmate Karen Britt and I sat with Bob in alternating shifts to relieve my sister. Bob asked me to please help him die. How is it that we as humans are forced to watch the ones we love suffer while our pets are euthanized to prevent their suffering?

Bob left our family profoundly affected by his death at the young age of 38. Exactly 90 days after his diagnosis, Bob was gone. He left behind a wife, a young daughter, and a son who would never know the dad he grew up to be so much like. Bob also left behind a family that was certain he knew beforehand that his time had come.

My sweet mother was an absolute angel in my life. She had a kindness about her that was unmatched by anyone I had ever known. Her kids were her life, and after we grew up and she retired early from the Federal Aviation Administration, she focused her loving attention on her grandkids. She often said children were gifts from God, and she cherished her time with her gifts. After Jill became a widow, Mama was instrumental in helping her get her life back on track, just as she was for my sister Tammy when she went through a divorce. Each of us always knew that we could find our strength in our mother when we couldn't find it in ourselves.

Once her grandkids started growing up and needing her attention less, she wanted to give her time in other ways. She was so excited to be able to help me with Care Advantage. She gushed with pride in me and the compassionate nature of my company so much that at times I could not help but be embarrassed. She never gave up her position of being my head cheerleader, and Care Advantage just gave her more to cheer about.

Mama started out with Care Advantage as a companion to a 92-year-old man I'll call "Mr. R." She loved her work, taking him to appointments, reading, and listening to him until the day he died. After that, Mama wanted to get more involved with office administration. She answered phones and had such a great mind for numbers that she also worked in accounting, where her mathematical abilities and her eye for detail kept everyone on their toes, whether they liked it or not.

Three years before her death, Mama suffered a heart attack due to anemia, related to her rheumatoid arthritis. I will never forget the call from my dad and my own racing heart as I heard him say, "Your mother had a heart attack." After just four short days, my mom was swiftly discharged from the hospital, and I would soon be reminded why I was led to start Care Advantage in the first place. Hours after she was released, my dad called frantically and said that Mom was having trouble breathing.

That time, my body raced 90 miles per hour with my racing heart to be by her side and assess the situation. As soon as I saw my mom, it was obvious to me that she was having congestive heart failure. I was so angry at the doctor and the hospital that had released her go home so sick—just like the many patients I had been instructed to discharge when I was a charge room nurse. For the purpose of freeing up her room to another paying patient, my mother's life was put in danger.

My mom and I had a rhythm between us. I could look at her and know when she was in trouble. Against my family members' wishes, who thought she was just tired, I had her admitted to a different hospital under the care of an intuitive cardiologist and dear friend of mine. After 10 days in this hospital, Mama was released in reasonably good health. This personal experience brought home my feeling that health care in this country stinks! If you don't have your own advocate watching over you, your life may be in grave danger—especially if you are left in the hands of medical professionals who are pushed by a reimbursement system that has nothing to do with patient care and is imposed on them by insurance companies.

Mama told everyone that I saved her life after that heart attack. Although I tried to get her to stop working and even held a retirement party for her, she insisted on coming to the office every day. I guess it was her therapy; she just loved being with people and making sure the job was done right.

Her final hospitalization came when I returned from a trip to New York. During that trip, I kept calling her to see if she needed to go to the hospital. I knew intuitively that something was wrong, and I could not get home fast enough. The moment I got back in town, I sped my way directly to see her. After one look, I took her straight to the hospital. But this time, she slid swiftly downhill. I guess we are all shrouded in some veil of denial when we are about to lose someone we thought surely would never die. I was in disbelief; my mom had always bounced back.

Three days before my mom's death, the nurse I hired to oversee her stay in the hospital called me at 6 a.m. to tell me Mom's mind was going. Again, I raced to be by her side. My mom began telling me a beautiful story—she was going to a wedding. She said she would be dancing and eating and she'd be very happy there. When I asked her if she would be marrying Dad, she immediately said, "No. It is not time for him." I wanted with all my heart not to believe what I knew to be true—the wedding my mother spoke of was her description of heaven.

Losing my mother was the most difficult experience of my life. I miss my head cheerleader, my angelic, sweet mom, every single day. When I received the 2009 Bernard Savage Award for community service—an award dedicated solely to me—I felt I should be so overwhelmed with happiness. Instead I felt an indescribable emptiness, a feeling that something was missing.

Tears filled my eyes when I realized that my greatest cheerleader in life was not there. She would have been so proud of me. Had she been alive, she would have bought zillions of newspapers and given the articles about the award to anyone breathing. Where once I would have been embarrassed by her enthusiasm for my success, I now felt only the void of not having her to cheer me on.

Great loss is one of those life lessons you hate getting. Even if it takes you to a higher plane of awareness or gratitude, it never seems to feel any better. Loss is loss, and it is a feeling you have to live with every day. I have dedicated my biggest award to my mom and co-wrote a song in her honor, but there is nothing yet that has been able to reduce the pain of her absence in my life. When I go to her grave and release balloons that my eyes follow for as long as I can see them, I feel I am sending my love to my mom—to the wedding in the sky.

Appreciate those who love you
like today is your last day together.

THE ABILITY TO GIVE AND RECEIVE LOVE IS A GIFT BEYOND MEASURE

CHAPTER THIRTEEN

A GOOD PROGNOSIS

I fully expect to wake up one day and not recognize the company that Buddy and I started over 20 years ago. My life was never the same after Care Advantage was born. But as far as the company has come, I believe there is so much farther for it to go.

It's one thing to start a business; it's quite another to watch it flourish beyond your wildest expectations. If anyone would have told me in nursing school that I would start and own a corporation with revenues in excess of $20 million, I can't imagine what my response would have been. I do know I would not have been able to put that response in writing on this page!

So where do we go from here? It has been said that "a test of a people is how it behaves toward the old. It is easy to love children. Even tyrants and dictators make a point of being fond of children. But the affection and care for the old, the incurable, the helpless are the true gold mines of a culture." Our society and how it cares for its people will soon be put to the test as the largest aging population ever is set to explode.

I am not worried about my company or any other well-run, compassion-based health care company—the prognosis is truly good for the profitability of the caregiving industry. What I am concerned about is the state of health care itself in this country; It is in the greatest turmoil ever—the whole system is broken. Insurance companies are still determining the care of patients through what treatments, procedures, and length of hospital stays will and will not be covered and by the methods used to reimburse health care providers. As a result, more and more people are sick and dying. Many are not getting the most effective treatment available when they need it and are being released too early from hospitals, thereby developing infections and other complications from surgeries once they are home. The fact that they are clueless about how to take care of themselves only compounds the problem. Trained home health care providers are required, now more than ever, and the situation is likely to get worse with an aging population explosion on the horizon.

The quality of hospital care, even in a country as advanced as the United States, is not at the level it should be. I would never have dreamed of allowing my mother to be without a private hospital nurse acting as her advocate after she almost died from congestive heart failure upon her early release. Families are in dire need of highly qualified advocates in hospitals to ensure that their loved ones are properly cared for. Hospitals are routinely understaffed, which causes their nurses and employees to be stressed, overworked, and constantly spread too thin. This translates into poor care for the patient. One small mistake can mean the difference between life and death for a loved one.

There are far more business startups in the home health field than when Care Advantage started in 1988, but unfortunately, many of those new businesses are not being started by someone schooled in health care like I was. Every Care Advantage office has nurses involved in running them. That distinction is important, considering that anyone from a shoe salesman to a college professor can decide to run a home health company, without any knowledge of the health care field or any compassion for the specialized needs of the elderly. Even excellent business people do not necessarily run quality health care companies. Unfortunately, any Tom, Dick, or Harriet can retain the licensure needed to start a home health care business today.

Still, the huge demand for services continually outpaces the supply of health care workers. This situation will only continue to get worse as the current population ages. So when I hear how unemployment is spinning out of control, I often wonder if wonder if people realize how many employment opportunities exist in the health care industry.

According to the Bureau of Labor and Statistics, the number of home health aides employed by the year 2016 will be 1,171,000—an increase of 49 percent over the year 2006. Many of these positions require program certification, rather than a four-year college degree. It is so important that people who enjoy caring for others make themselves aware of the many opportunities in the health care field. To that end, a table of sample health careers, educational requirements, and potential salaries can be found at www.heartknocks.net.

Being a nurse is one of the most rewarding careers in the world. It is a flexible career that works for any lifestyle and can take you to any part of the world you want to go. Like my daddy told me long ago—there will always be jobs for nurses. There are so many opportunities to uplift and inspire on a daily basis, and more love is always received than is given away. Compassion is needed in every possible arena of care, but nursing shortages are still rampant. Many nurses are simply too tired to do the work they love with an attitude that is required to do the job well. Often that challenge gives patients and their families the mistaken belief that the nurses on staff don't care about doing a good job for them. The real problem is that we need more nurses!

Good nursing candidates must be motivated to enter the field, which is one of the main reasons I so strongly support our local community college program for nursing at J. Sargeant Reynolds. The quarter-million-dollar endowment fund established in my name will provide the college with needed funds to improve its nursing school curriculum and enable it to award more scholarships to deserving nursing candidates. I do not want one motivated individual who wants to be a nurse to miss their calling. America cannot afford for that to happen.

As a generation of baby boomers age, the health profession must be prepared for all the opportunities to serve. Many people in the boomer age group, having decided not to have children, will find themselves alone with no one to care for them in their older years. For them, home health care will not be a luxury, but a vital necessity. Home health improves the quality of life and general happiness of seniors and is set to experience huge growth over the next few decades, when the elderly population is on target to exceed 70 million people!

Our longevity at Care Advantage gives us the privilege of being one of the most recognized names in the home health field. But to continue to grow as a company, we have to keep moving forward with new ideas for expanding our capacity and our vision. We have to look ahead of the curve to continue to compete in an industry constantly in flux.

With a four-year plan to double the company's revenues, we have our work cut out for us. But a short-sighted vision will net us a plan that is likely to underestimate our potential and leave us unprepared for the coming growth in customer demand.

While focusing on geographical expansion and opportunities that will help us "get rich in our niche," Care Advantage will have to use its human capital wisely to succeed. Margins of operation will seek improvement through automation of key processes, and new leadership development programs will assist us in growing the strongest candidates to lead us in new directions.

As it expands, Care Advantage will inevitably move away from its entrepreneurial roots toward a more corporate-oriented environment. It will no doubt be an exciting time for the company as we prepare to grow up with the baby boomer generation.

As for me on a personal level, the opportunities seem endless. Entrepreneurs are visionaries. We see the big picture and dream the dreams that others are afraid to dream. Creativity is where my passion lies; it is my medicine. That's why there eventually comes a time in most every entrepreneur's life when their mature business needs a fresh set of eyes to continue the company on a growth pattern. I have a chief operations officer who is everything that I am not, and that is a perfect scenario for me and for the company. With Tripp Perrin's operational leadership, I am confident that Care Advantage will soar to new heights, not even imagined by me. It's already starting!

Surrounding myself with highly qualified and loyal members of my family and by placing dedicated and able people that I have known for a very long time in key company positions, I am able to stretch my wings in many directions. As my dreams continue to grow, I have many creative projects currently under way, including a song I co-wrote in honor of the undying love between my mother and father. "The One You Just Can't Live Without" is currently awaiting its big break with the right artist in the country music industry.

I feel so blessed to have been able to share my heart with a little corner of the world. I have given and received love in large doses from all directions over the years. Who could ask for more than that? The Parable of The Talents in the Bible always held special meaning for me. When we are blessed with talents, we are to use them to multiply and do good things in the world; otherwise we squander our gifts and risk losing them altogether.

It has been my sincere hope in taking on this book project that my story will inspire others to live the life of their dreams, one of meaning. For when we do that, we make the world a better place for all of us. In telling my story, I also intend to advance my life's mission to give back to the field of nursing a measure of the good it has given to me. To that end, a percentage of every copy of this book that is sold will be donated to nursing and health care scholarships at nursing schools and community colleges to assist in the education and training of those with a heartfelt passion to care for others.

> *Passion is the spark*
> *that lights a fire under Purpose.*
>
> ## OH, THE PLACES YOU'LL GO!
> –Dr. Seuss

CHAPTER FOURTEEN

YOUR CHECKUP

So far this book has been all about me—*my* business, *my* life, *my* dreams. Now it's time to put the spotlight on you! What did you hope to come away with by choosing to spend your time reading about *my* life? Let's talk about *your* life.

Are you following your dreams—or are they following behind you, waiting for you to wake up and create your best life? If you had an appointment with the Dream Genie tomorrow, would you have a clear vision of what to ask for? Some of you would, but unfortunately, I bet many of you would not.

The good news for you is that I did not have my dream life all mapped out in the beginning either. But I did have a vision of the life I wanted to end up with. How I got to that life began with a problem, whose solution led to an idea, which became a business, that made me the CEO of a company worth millions. If it can happen to me, it can happen to you!

So let's get started on your dream checkup. It's time to set your intention to focus on the life of your dreams—the one you would choose to have if you knew beyond all doubt that it was yours for the taking.

Success Principle Number One:

....

Imagine the life your dreams are made of.

The only way to envision the life you want to have sometime in the future is to see it detailed in your mind's eye in the present; for that, you will need to engage your imagination. You must be able to visualize images of the best life you can imagine for yourself as if it were already here, whether it is one you create on your own or one you model after the life of someone you admire.

Our dreams are usually created from our experiences in life, and sometimes we do not even realize when we have latched on to a dream for ourselves. That was probably true for me. I held on to the vision of abundance I experienced when I was about 10 on a visit to the Ukrop family farm. They were very successful as owners of a chain of local grocery stores even then, but that was not the part of the picture that grabbed my attention.

What impressed me as a little girl was the visual of their huge family farm with a beautiful lake! Every year when the church picnic was held at their farm, there were humongous displays of food to share with their friends and family. THAT was the life I wanted! It is my earliest recollection of a vision for my life, and it was imaged long before I became a nurse.

If I had not learned by now how dreams become reality, I would consider it a major miracle that after choosing a career in nursing, I ended up as the CEO of a chain of home health care businesses known for giving back to the communities they serve, very much along the same lines as the Ukrop's grocery chain! In many respects, the earliest vision of my best life came true for me!

Can you think of a dream you held as a child? Did you picture the house of your dreams, or the car or career of a lifetime? You have to know where you want to end up before the "how-to" thoughts can show up to get you there. And my advice to you is to dream BIG! It is just as easy to dream big as it is to dream small—so go for it!

Heart Hint:
Begin with the end in mind.

Success Principle Number Two:

....

Recognize the idea that inspires excitement.

Let's talk about the spark of inspiration called an idea. All day long, ideas are popping in and out of your mind. Sometimes you get one that takes you by surprise and really makes you think. You start feeling all excited—maybe you even get goose bumps! That's the one that deserves your full attention. Your feelings are a reflection of your state of mind, and if the energetic vibration of your body has been raised by the thought of a particular idea, you would do well to listen to it.

I had that experience as a charge room nurse. After noticing how many people went home sick from the hospital after a short stay, I could not help but wonder what would happen to them without knowledgeable care. What happened next is important:

I thought that a nurse should be checking in on them at home. It's not that I immediately concluded, "Oh, what a great business idea. I am going to start a home health care company and become a millionaire." That notion was the farthest thing from my mind. Like most people, I had no clue of where my thoughts would go, if anywhere. I also had no idea at the time that there is a specific intelligence in the birth and nourishment of an idea.

But, as a nurse, I could not stop thinking about the sick patients going home from the hospital. I was curious and concerned about them, and my mind kept drifting back to the situation that was occurring every day in my life as a nurse.

There is a universal law that basically states, Where you place your *attention* will be perceived as your *intention* by a power greater than us. If you focus on something long enough, sooner or later, you can expect to see change coming from those thoughts.

Heart Hint:
Notice what you notice.

Success Principle Number Three:

....

Keep your idea under wraps while considering its potential.

A lot of people have difficulty holding on to an idea once they start hearing all the reasons why it won't work. Somehow the disbelievers have a way of stripping away all the confidence originally generated by the idea in the dreamer's mind before it popped out of the womb of thought into the scary world.

However, I have to admit that I've never had a big problem telling others about my ideas, because I am usually able to ignore the negative influences of other people. In fact, negative feedback often increases my persistence and makes me determined to see my idea succeed. Most of the time I'm able to gather endless amounts of support when I share my ideas with others. Maybe they see the excitement in my face and can't deny the possibility of success. No matter what attitude you find in your circle of influence, once you are on top of making things happen, people will start believing in you, increasing your belief in yourself and creating a snowball effect in your success rate.

As a nurse, I have always had the advantage of being part of a large field of comrades, who would thrill to see one of their own succeed. But in the very beginning, the well-meaning naysayers showed up in numbers to discourage me from "ruining my life" with my idea about a new career in home health.

Mark Victor Hansen and Robert Allen, in their book "The One Minute Millionaire," say that every idea is born dying. That is because of all the people who want to tell you why your thinking is misguided. Many times these are the very people you think will want the best for you, like family and close friends. They are trying to protect you with their cautionary tales and doubts. But in essence they are attempting to wrap you in the cocoon of their own fear, which is the only reality they know. Unfortunately, it can be so easy to believe them when you don't have all the answers to how you'll get your idea off the ground. That is why I strongly recommend you err on the side of caution when your idea is fresh and vulnerable, and be selective about who you share your dreams with.

Another problem with spilling your beans to the world when you are all excited about the possibilities is that you risk losing the energy that is generating your feelings of excitement. That is a form of self-sabotage. Often, just telling everyone about your idea is enough of an emotional high to burn out every spark of inspiration it holds. The energy needed to motivate you to take the next step can be lost in the repetitive telling of the dream.

The best plan for handling all of the excitement that is swirling around in your head is to share it with a few like-minded people who can hold the vision for you. A well-known practice of the world's most successful people is to create a mastermind group of inspiring people who meet regularly to support and magnify each other's beliefs. The secret is to stay as far away from the naysayers and energy vampires as possible, because they will waste no time sucking all the blood right out of your idea and your life, if you let them.

Heart Hint:
Sh-h-h-h-h!

Success Principle Number Four:

Begin to take baby steps to explore the possibilities.

Everyone would love to be able to wiggle their nose and have everything instantly occur the way they want it like Elizabeth Montgomery did when she starred on "Bewitched" many moons ago. If only it were that easy! Nothing happens without exerting effort in the correct way. One of the great thinkers of the nineteenth century, Henry David Thoreau, said, "If one advances confidently in the direction of one's dreams, and endeavors to live the life which one has imagined, one will meet with success unexpected in common hours."

That is so beautifully worded and it's wonderful advice, but to be able to follow Thoreau's wisdom, we must have a clear picture in our mind of the dream we want before we can move toward it. The problem for most of us is that we have not been trained to imagine a big life or to even recognize the makings of a dream when it shows up. That is why it is not only important to pay attention to the feelings that accompany new ideas but to explore the possibilities in them, even before we know that we could be headed in the direction of our dreams. I surely did not know in my own case.

Unfortunately, many ideas rarely advance past the thinking stage to the doing phase. Often, owners of great ideas do not take even the smallest of steps beyond the thought realm to move their ideas toward reality. My dad is a perfect example. He had so many great ideas that he never acted on. He wanted to open a restaurant and a campground in Nags Head, North Carolina. He also talked for hours about starting his own business as an electrician. But he never took a single step in the direction of his dreams. He just didn't believe he could make any of them work. As a result, he ended up with a life of woulda, coulda, shoulda, instead of the one he really wanted for himself. He asked me so many times, "Debbie, what makes you so different? How did you accomplish more than anyone else in the family?" There was a lesson for me in my daddy's inaction. I learned to roll like a ball. I didn't over-think my ideas; I just kept moving with them.

Action is as important to the nourishment of an idea as thought was for the idea to be created. As Stretton Smith says in one of his 4T prosperity lessons, "Life is a buffet; you have to get up and serve yourself." Consider that someone had the idea for creating the clothes you are wearing. But if someone hadn't taken appropriate action to have them designed, manufactured, and marketed to you, they would still be an idea in someone's head instead of the clothes on your back.

My first step in exploring my thoughts about a solution for sick patients at home was a small one—I checked the newspaper to see if there were any home health opportunities in the area. I was surprised to find a company operating locally and looking for a marketing representative. When I looked into the company, I knew it could potentially provide me with the information and experience I needed to further consider the problem of patient care. Home health aftercare made sense to me, even though I had no clue of how it would all pan out in the end. That brings to mind another issue for consideration— the *how* to make it happen.

We do not need to know the order of how things will go in the pursuit of a dream. Sometimes, we may not even recognize that we are on the right track early in the game. We simply need to keep the thought or idea alive while detaching from a specific outcome. Our job is to just follow our gut instincts and keep moving. Eventually, you will begin to see teachers, supporters, and opportunities showing up in your life that seem like coincidences to help you. Your biggest responsibility, then, is to recognize these gifts and be open to receive them when they show up.

Heart Hint:
Right action brings ideas into reality.

Success Principle Number Five:

. . . .

Be willing to take a risk to bring your idea into being.

After finding a job opportunity in the newspaper, I did something that most people have a great deal of trouble with—I took a risk. Was I apprehensive? Of course, I was. But I knew I had tapped into a real problem in patient care, and I was looking for a solution. My curiosity to see if private care would be a viable option for the marketplace loomed large. This position would let me test-drive the solution while still collecting an income. It would also give me experience I would not be able to receive in a hospital setting, where the problem was being created.

Leaving the security of my nursing position to venture back out into the job market for a new career in health care sales would end up broadening my skills, along with my horizons, over time. It would also confirm my idea about home health. But these are all benefits I would discover in time. They were not built into my decision to leave. My decision to leave was part of my single-minded purpose to explore a potential solution to the problem. It has been said that the solution to a problem is never found at the thought-level of the problem. So even though everyone around me was creating as much fear as possible surrounding my intention to leave, I stepped out boldly and made the change.

A Course in Miracles states that there are only two emotions in existence—love and fear. Love causes your feelings to expand, making you happy and exhilarated. Fear causes your feelings to contract and constrict, making you anxious, questioning, and out of sorts. The wide range of all other feelings experienced come from one of these two emotions. In fear, you will backtrack the path to your decision and second-guess everything about it. Fear shows up as worry and procrastination. It clothes itself in apathy, doubt, and indecision. Fear can create enough caution in your mind to stop the lifeblood from flowing, and it can stop a dream or an idea dead in its tracks.

In order to continue advancing toward the best life you can imagine, you must hold firm in your beliefs and resist the temptation to allow the influence of negative thinking and self-doubt to sneak into your consciousness and rob you of the validity of your idea. When you keep your thoughts positive and expectant, you will resonate with positive energy flow, and your ideas will keep moving your dreams in a forward direction. The last thing you want to do is to allow fear and cynicism to disable you and your best life by dismantling your desires and your purpose.

Heart Hint:
Step boldly into the fear.

Success Principle Number Six:

....

Always follow your instincts.

It might surprise some business people to know that Napoleon Hill named the sixth sense as the final principle to becoming rich in his famous book, "Think and Grow Rich." It was so important to the formula of how the most successful people in America achieved greatness and became wealthy that he said every one of the other 12 principles were simply "lead ins to the understanding and acceptance of this key principle," which he said must be mastered to succeed. Gut instincts, intuition, divine guidance and hunches are other words referring to the same thing—strong feelings of inner knowing that when acted upon will take you in the direction of your highest good.

After I had worked with the home health care company for a while, I began to think and feel that I had learned enough to take the concept of home health aftercare back to the hospital setting. I planned to sell the idea to the administrators based on my positive experience in the marketplace. I had also made a lot of new friends and picked up a wealth of contacts that would help me if I needed them. I had a hunch that my idea would go over well at the hospital; I was right about that. What I didn't know was that this would be the crossroads in my journey that would lead me directly to the dream life I had imagined for myself.

So how does one recognize intuition? Did you ever find yourself struggling over a multiple-choice test question? You'd go back and forth over the decision about which answer to pick. Then, when you finally chose one—or worse, changed your original answer to a different one—you found out from a friend that your first choice was the right one all along. This annoying little scenario is known as second-guessing, and it was your intuition or inner knowing that your ego mind was fighting with. It's when you go into your head to analyze the choice given to you by the still, small voice within you. Everyone hears the voice, but until one learns to trust and follow the voice of intuition, things will not work out as well as they could.

I have a very good sense of inner direction. The expansive high-energy feeling surrounding my thoughts always directs the best way for me to go. When I feel any sense of foreboding, I head in the opposite direction. I rarely defy my instincts, and I am rarely wrong. I know immediately when I am on the right path. I feel serene and at peace. Everything works out in my best interest, almost like magic—big things and little things.

A simple example occurred last Thanksgiving, when my family started a small football pool. I do not watch football or know anything about the teams, players, or their records, so obviously my picks came from some other source. When I won the pool, my over analytical, football-educated male family members were in utter disbelief! They would probably prefer to believe it was my "King Midas touch" that brought me the gold rather than my keen sense of intuition. But I have seen it too many times not to recognize it.

Even if you don't feel you have good instincts or intuition, this ability can be developed through the practice of meditation. It is a fact that intuition lies within each of us. To access the power of the subconscious mind and the guidance of the infinite power, you must go within. Napoleon Hill said, "Through the aid of the sixth sense, you will be warned of impending dangers in time to avoid them and notified of opportunities in time to embrace them."

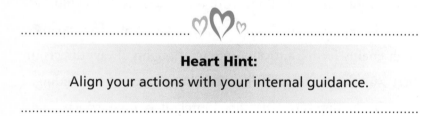

Heart Hint:
Align your actions with your internal guidance.

Success Principle Number Seven:

....

Recognize the opportunities in adversity.

The title of this book was no accident. I am sure you understood that "The School of *Heart* Knocks" was a play on words for "The School of *Hard* Knocks." I acknowledge that my life has been nowhere near as hard as some, but it has certainly had its share of adversity. I've taken quite a few hard knocks to my heart. But I am amazed at how many opportunities came directly from the hardships I thought were insurmountable at the time. How things turned out put a whole new spin on pain!

Even being adopted was actually a blessing. It was the *need to be adopted* that left the stain of being unwanted on my self-worth. Growing up with the knowledge that your biological parents were willing to give you away can make you feel not good enough. I always felt I had to prove myself worthy of being a Johnston. But from that emotional turmoil grew an inner determination to be the best at everything I attempted. No one would work harder than me to be the perfect child. My motivation for perfection spilled over into adulthood, and it drove me to apply my nursing skills to the business arena and to use my compassion for others in pain.

After bringing home health back to a hospital setting, I thought I had accomplished what I had set out to do. Sick patients were being taken care of, and I had created a purpose-filled position for myself far beyond what I would have been able to achieve as a charge room nurse. So imagine my defeated feelings when the administrator of the hospital pulled a fast one and took my idea, along with the division I created! I admit that I could not see one bright spot in that decision for me. I also could not see that because of his actions, a prosperous home health business of my own was on the horizon.

It's almost impossible to recognize opportunity when it is cloaked in adversity. The key is to learn to expect something good to emerge from whatever challenge comes your way on the journey. Accept the fact that there are often temporary setbacks needed for adjustments to your life's plan that you are not entirely privy to, so you will be more accepting of them and less affected *by* them when they show up. Many times, out of those difficulties, come the turning points in your life.

According to Reverend Michael Beckwith, "You will be pushed by pain until you are pulled by a vision." If you remain focused on the pain within the challenge, tucking your tail between your legs or struggling against the adversity to have what *you think* should be happening, you may miss an even greater opportunity in the making. Remember, there are no pearls to be found in oysters where there is no grit to grind.

I was devastated when my cheating husband took away the opportunity for me to have my own baby. But the pain from that setback fueled an intense desire to create a vision of success that I did not know I was even capable of. My company became the baby I was able to create for myself. I believe it is highly unlikely that I would own a company worth millions had adversity not shown up along the way. If things had gone as I had planned, I would still be working for someone else, and I would not have been able to realize the life of my dreams or help others as I have in the process.

It is with that knowledge that I can honestly thank my ex-husband. I realize that the pain I suffered through our relationship lifted me to my higher purpose in life. Though we rarely communicate these days, I am still close to his family and feel blessed to be able to have lunch often with his special mother, whom I love. I have learned with time that love, like life, can take us in directions we had not planned to go. We all make mistakes; no one is perfect. With all sincerity, I wish my ex-husband the very best of luck in his medical practice and, above all, I wish him the joy of real love in his life.

Heart Hint:
Look for the silver lining cloaked in darkness.

Success Principle Number Eight:

....

Consult a close advisor whom you trust.

No matter how simple or complicated your plan or idea is, you will need someone you respect and trust as an advisor at some point in your process of becoming successful. This person may be a mentor who has specialized knowledge in a particular area of interest to you, it may be an accountant or attorney with wise business advice to protect you, or it may be a friend who can see for you what you cannot see for yourself.

Luckily for me, I had someone who filled all three roles. Buddy served as my friend, mentor, and wise counsel. It was a huge turning point when I went to see him for advice about the hospital administrator who began withholding my bonus money. If this challenge had not been presented to me, I would not have sought out my friend's advice, in which case starting my own business may never have occurred to me. You, too, may need someone who has a greater vision for you than you have for yourself; someone who believes in you enough to push you when you refuse to believe that you are capable enough or worthy enough for what they suggest for you.

So many times in life opportunities show up, and because we are not ready emotionally or mentally to receive them, we miss our chance. Most of the time, we have not been taught that we are worthy to receive. We are taught to be polite in a self-reliant kind of way. Can you hear yourself saying "No thank you" to something someone is offering that you'd love to have? It is often hard for most of us to accept something as simple as a compliment. Do you remember disagreeing with someone when they told you how nice you looked or what a great smile you have? These are little bits of proof that it is uncomfortable for us to accept gifts from other people. We must cultivate the ability to receive.

Often we define ourselves by belief systems accumulated over a lifetime from experiences that were less than worthy of us. I could not see the entrepreneur Buddy could see in me. But fortunately, Buddy refused to accept my "No thank you" to his vision for me. Since he didn't give up on the vision, I eventually gave in to it. That is the type of person everyone should have on the road to the top.

Don't let your vision of yourself confine you to your definition of who you think you are or what you think is possible for you. Your fears hold you back with worries of failure and obstacles as you try to envision yourself on a higher path. Even though most of what you worry about will never happen, those worries have the potential of robbing you of your future. That's why it is so important to have a mastermind group or someone whose opinion you respect to help you consider new and more expansive roles for yourself. When you are able to do this, you can step up to a life of bigger dreams than previously imagined—dreams worthy of the life you deserve.

Heart Hint:
Be open to receive new ideas.

Success Principle Number Nine:

Live an attitude of gratitude.

Never allow yourself to think you are so important or so special that you fail to have a grateful heart. It would be hard for me *not* to be grateful when I remember that I actually slept in a dresser drawer as a child because my parents couldn't afford a bed. When I look at my life now in comparison to my meager beginnings, I am simply amazed and overwhelmed by feelings of gratitude, followed quickly by disbelief. I appreciate the fact that my parents loved me enough to scrape together the money to give me an excellent education that became the catalyst to change my life. And I am so very grateful that I could give back to them in this lifetime.

According to the famous Roman philosopher Cicero, "Gratitude is not only the greatest of virtues, but the parent of all the others." Gratitude is not a way to think; it is a way *to be*. Being in gratitude is the fastest way to release frustrations and worry and switch over to expansive feelings of joy. When you are able to do that, you change your thought frequency to a higher level of vibration, enabling you to attract to you things that you desire. A consciousness of gratitude also brings you serenity and peace of mind—necessities for the best life you could possibly live. No amount of wealth can give you peace of mind without gratitude. I learned a lot about gratitude from the Unity Church way of living and the spiritual principles I found through it.

Giving back goes hand-in-hand with gratitude. Giving is one of the best gifts you can receive. I know that sounds a little backward, but it's true. It is so much fun to be able to give to others and help them in ways I could not have done without the financial means to do it. I am reminded of the time I let my dad drive my new Lexus. He was complaining about his car, and I asked him if he wanted to have the Lexus. I was shocked when he said "Yes!" I couldn't believe I was going to have to give my car to my dad, but it felt so good to be able to afford to do it. Being able to share my success with my family and friends is one of the things I am most grateful for; it has made my journey a more worthwhile one. Taking my nieces and nephew and their friends on trips to Europe was rewarding to me. Organizing a family cruise and paying everyone's way was rewarding to me. Being able to care for my sister with multiple sclerosis and see that she has the best life possible, under the circumstances, is rewarding to me.

I believe, too, with all my heart that we are meant to share our good and help pull the next person up the ladder of success. I was able to set up one of my former employees in a business of his own, running his first group home. He now has eight of those homes, and we call him "Money-making Matt." He recently bought the car of his dreams and is so full of joy and appreciation for the opportunity to be able to run his own company. But if the truth be known, the real gift was in the giving; how blessed I feel for being in a position to help him. You can never give without getting back more than you gave. That's why giving is such a gift!

Never get so big that you forget those who helped you get where you are. Care Advantage shares its profits with its employees. It recognizes hard work and makes life more fun with contests that reward winners with trips. I always try to give my employees life-expanding experiences they may not have been able to give themselves.

We have appreciation parties for our clients; one time we hired buses and took them around town on a Tacky Light Tour during the Christmas season. We honestly put thankfulness in every area of our business. Every effort is made to give love and kindness to our patients and treat them like family. We are not always perfect, but as they say, "It's not for a lack of trying."

Care Advantage gives back to the communities in which it operates. We support non-profits and nursing scholarships, and give smiles to children with cleft palates. We spend time at Comfort Zone Camp, an organization for children struggling with grief, and give loyal support to other organizations for children, such as the Make-A-Wish Foundation and Big Brothers Big Sisters. We give to research organizations that work to discover cures for illnesses, such as the Arthritis Foundation, the MS Society, Massey Cancer Center, American Cancer Society,

Susan G. Komen for the Cure, and the Cullather Brain Center for patients with brain tumors.

My company does a lot of good things, because I lead with and follow my heart. My company is all about heart—a grateful heart. The sign on my door says, "Good Business Sense comes from the Heart," and it is my intention to live that belief. It's about helping the world be a little bit better because we can.

That's what you can do by being all that you can be. One person can make a difference by living life with an attitude of gratitude—why not you?

And you say, "Well, sure, I will......when I have as much money as you....... when my ship comes in, like yours did." Here's a secret that will rock your world, if you let it. It will take faith and a belief in something bigger than yourself to accept this little gift I am about to share with you. Are you open to receive it so it can make a difference in your life? Ready or not, here it is:

. . . .

You have to begin living your life with an attitude of gratitude *before* you think you have a big reason to be grateful; *before* your ship comes in.

. . . .

Yes, you heard me right; keyword—*before*! Remember, you have to begin with the end in mind. You must start by being grateful for the wonderful things you already have. See in your mind's eye the life you will be even more grateful for, but live like you already have it—in gratitude! In "Think and Grow Rich"—one of the most highly acclaimed books about becoming successful in business—Napoleon Hill said, "It is essential to give before you get." Now, that is not to say that you have the self-centered motivation of giving *to* get, because that mindset won't get you where you want to be. Giving in gratitude for what you do have will create a shift in your mind to a feeling of joy. That joy will enable you to raise your body's level of vibration so that you can create the life you want.

One way I live this principle of giving in gratitude is by tithing a full 10 percent of all that I receive to the place I am spiritually fed. I do this without wavering, and I have done so consistently since I took the 4T Prosperity Program years ago in the midst of great emotional pain. Tithing is a universal law. It is as functional as gravity and affects you whether you believe it or not—just like gravity. I give in joy, and from the moment I started to live that principle in my life, money has rolled in like a river.

That's my little secret of success. And if you look at other extremely successful people, you will probably find that it's their little secret, too.

Heart Hint:
Move forward by giving back.

Success Principle Number Ten:

....

LOVE like there is no tomorrow!

If you go through life and somehow end up more successful and wealthier than anyone has ever been before, but you don't have love in your life—you have failed to become all that you could be. Life is about love. The emotions evoked by feelings of love and gratitude cause other negative and harmful emotions to dissipate and lose their influence. Love is spiritual and connects you with your divine nature. Having a true loving relationship is as close to spiritual nirvana as you will ever come; whether it is platonic or romantic does not matter. Recently, I saw this principle unfold before my eyes like the dewy petals of a rosebud after a summer shower.

Ever since my mother died, my dad decided to give up on his life, too. It was almost too much sadness to witness. No matter what I, or any of my siblings, tried to do for him, his spirits could not be lifted for long. He visited my mother's grave far too often and grieved her absence in his life far too much. It was his unhappiness that provoked me to write the sad song about his lonely life without her. I even created a non-profit organization in honor of my mom called Eunice's Circle of Friends where lonely hearts could get together to meet and have fun. But my dad did not have fun.

Just about the time this book was being finished, my dad was hospitalized with a shoulder replacement. At first, that seemed to make everything even worse. The man who had taken care of both my mother and his own mother didn't want anyone to have to take care of him. I had all but resigned myself to the belief that my dad was going to get his wish and leave us much sooner than he needed through his powerful hope of dying. We hired a nurse to look after him, hoping for a recovery. What we got instead was a miracle!

This nurse was an angel. She and my dad seemed like perfect companions. My dad said that no one had ever taken care of him like she had. Sometimes love comes through healing, although I am not sure if it was his shoulder or his heart that was being healed faster. In an instant, everything changed.

This caring individual did for our dad what none of his children could do for him. Perhaps, without fully realizing it, she had breathed new life into his heart. Suddenly, dad had a new lease on life.

To an outside observer, it would appear that the Rip Van Winkle asleep in my dad's soul was waking up from a long deep slumber. He whispered to me one day, "Debbie, have you noticed how I'm alive again?" I had been afraid to say a word. I just smiled through big tears of happiness for him. I was so overjoyed at how my dad finally opened up his eyes to the blessings before him. He may have missed out on a few business opportunities earlier in his life, but he did not miss out on the most important opportunity of his life. He chose to believe in possibilities and in his ability to feel again, and in doing so, he chose to live. I am so proud of my dad. I want to be just like him when I grow up!

Love is an emotion powerful enough to put you on a creative plane of thought from which masterpieces are made and empires are built. Never underestimate the power of love in your life and in your success. It is a known fact that the two things most entrepreneurs suffer from are a lack of health and a lack of healthy relationships. Both of these maladies can be remedied with love.

It may surprise you to know that Napoleon Hill also found out through his 20 years of research that some of the most successful people you have ever heard of did not hit the peak of their success until they experienced genuine feelings of desire that come with true love and romance. The affect of love on the brain has been said to awaken a sleeping giant within, because the emotions connected to love serve to stimulate the creative genius needed for greatness.

So if you thought burning the midnight oil alone in your office every night was getting you ahead in the business world or closer to your riches—think again!

Heart Hint:

Success is better when shared with love.

CONCLUSION

You can see that the creation of my health care company was a journey. The idea that became my business was not recognized as a flash of inspiration, nor did my success happen overnight. But remember, it didn't take a lifetime either—and that was *before* I found out how dreams are made! Hopefully, at this point, you have a better idea of how to get a head start on the path to your best life. It's never too late!

Unbeknownst to me, the success leg of my life journey began when I noticed a health care problem that needed a solution. My passion for patient care kept my attention on the issue. I was a nurse, and I cared about what happened to people. It did not resonate with my skills as a charge room nurse to release the sick to go home and do for themselves what nurses had been trained to do for them. It was obvious to me that those patients needed help at home, and that they were not going to be getting it.

However, just as we do not always know when we have stepped on the path that will lead us to our dream life, we also do not know what the outcome of a particular thought or idea will be. We must have faith that there is a higher power and that all will be clear when it is time. I did not try to figure out the patient care problem in my head; I simply listened to my instincts and followed where they led me. My constant attention to my thoughts brought opportunities and people that eventually allowed me to find a solution to the problem and gave me the dream life I had imagined years ago as a little girl on the Ukrop's farm. At the time, I could never have imagined how it would all turn out.

I think my life illustrates how important it is to listen to the still small voice inside you, and when an idea or thought pervades your mind and holds special meaning for you, stick with it. Every idea or thought may not have the potential to change your life, but wouldn't you hate to miss the one that could, simply because you did not notice it or give it time to develop? I cannot stress enough the importance of paying attention to your thoughts.

You are the creator of your life. Mary Morrissey, a gifted speaker, best-selling author, and a world leader in the human potential movement, says that everything is created twice—once in someone's mind as a thought and then in the world as the physical manifestation of that thought. My thoughts to change the way patients were cared for became gold for myself and others around me—yours can, too, if you nurture them.

Andrew Carnegie's secret of success was explained this way, "All achievement, all earned riches have their beginning in an idea." I began this book talking about ideas. I hoped I might inspire someone, somewhere to turn an idea into a multi-million-dollar dream of a lifetime. I can't help but wonder if that someone might be you.

By now you should know that the answer to the question depends...

It depends on your answer to the question.

Recommended Reading to Retain a Prosperous Mindset:

Think and Grow Rich .... Napoleon Hill

The Science of Getting Rich .... Wallace Wattles

Building Your Field of Dreams .... Mary Morrissey

Spiritual Economics .... Eric Butterworth

I've Always Looked Up to Giraffes .... Hugh Gouldthorpe

Money and the Law of Attraction .... Esther and Jerry Hicks

Excuse Me, Your Life is Waiting .... Lynn Grabhorn

The One Minute Millionaire .... Mark Victor Hansen,
Robert Allen

Prosperity Programs:

The 4T Prosperity Program .... Stretton Smith

Prosperity Plus .... Mary Morrissey

A WORD
ABOUT ADOPTION

Childhood is a playground for lessons that will be revisited many times before you define your purpose in your life. Often what happens in your earliest memories has a way of casting shadows over your whole life. Adoption was a huge shadow for me, as it is for a vast number of people who find out at some point in their lives that they are not the sons or daughters of the parents who are raising them. My story is a perfect example of the pain of abandonment, for that is what adoption first feels like.

Even though adoption was a lesson that made me more determined to succeed, it was still a debilitating factor in my life of personal relationships. I had learned that people I expected to love me would leave me, and issues of trust would color my perception of potential mates. I chose partners who were not capable of being available to me and who would disappoint me just as my subconscious mind had taught me to expect.

But, with time, I have learned something invaluable that I would like to share with anyone who may have issues with their own adoption and possibly harbor feelings of low self-worth because of it. We have the ability to choose our perception of a situation, and as with most things in life, there are two ways to look at everything.

As a nurse, I was once witness to a new mother who had decided that it would be best for all concerned to give her newborn up for adoption. Once the baby had been delivered, the mother asked to see her baby. The attending doctor was unusually cruel as he refused her request, telling her there was no reason for her to see a baby that she had decided to give away. Experiencing that new mother's deep pain and sadness gave me a different perspective of my own situation. It is often an act of love and courage for a mother to give up a part of herself that she has nourished within her own body for nine months. I thought about my birth mother and couldn't help but wonder if she had felt such pain in giving me up.

We cannot know why things happen the way they do, but I have come to know that my adoption was a blessing of the highest order for me. I absolutely know I would not have had many of the opportunities in life that have been afforded me had things not gone just the way they did. My parents were the best. They loved me with full hearts and helped mold me into the person I have become.

> THE MOST IMPORTANT LESSON IN THE LIFETIME JOURNEY OF THE ADOPTED CHILD IS TO LEAVE BEHIND THE ASSOCIATED SCARS OF ABANDONMENT AND EMBRACE THE BEAUTIFUL CONCEPT OF BEING CHOSEN.

"One of the deep secrets of life is that all that is really worth the doing is what we do for others."

The following letter from my sweet mom means so much to me that I have it framed and displayed where I can read it everyday. It reminds me of the many special times we were able to have in our life together as a family; I am so grateful for every single one of them. The thought of her getting out of bed and recounting those memories is a blessing beyond measure.

12-18-03

Dear Debbie,

It's 4:00 in the morning and I couldn't sleep so I thought I would chat with you.

I went to a Hall Mark store + spent awhile looking for a very very special card for you — they haven't made it yet

Thanks for All and Everything you have done for us. We have enjoyed alot of Wonderful Trips, a car, New Furniture the very special Anniversary party — the Beautiful clothes + money. What more could anyone ask for. You are our Guardian

ANGEL.

OVER THE YEARS YOU
HAVE ALWAYS BEEN THERE
FOR US ALL. YOU SEEM TO
KNOW WHATS BEST EVEN
IF WE DON'T SEEM TO
APPRECIATE YOU.

YOUR DAYS ARE ALWAYS
BUSY + STRESSFUL BUT YOU
ALWAYS HANDLE THINGS SO
WELL. DO WISH WE COULD
DO SOMETHING EXTRA SPECIAL
FOR YOU. YOU DESERVE IT!

WE ALL HAVE ENJOYED
YOUR BEAUTIFUL ESTATE ON
THE JAMES. WE HAVE SO
MANY MEMORIES TO HANG
ON TO.

I ESPECIALLY WANT TO
THANK YOU FOR THE QUALITY
OF TIME + THE LOVE YOU

HAVE SHARED WITH ME. THIS
WORLD IS A BETTER PLACE
CAUSE YOUR IN IT.

I'M VERY GRATEFUL TO
GOD THAT HE TRUSTED ME TO
RAISE 6 CHILDREN — I FELT
SO BLESSED, NOW I HAVE
GOTTEN OLDER + MY FAMILY
IS SO VERY WONDERFUL TO
HAVE AROUND,

IN CLOSING I JUST
WANT TO SAY I REALLY DO
APPRECIATE YOU + ALL YOU
HAVE DONE FOR ALL OF US

Love Always!
Mom

ACKNOWLEDGMENTS

There are so many people that have been blessings in my life, and I wish I could mention every single one of them, but there are not enough pages in this book to do so. However, there are some who must be singled out for the huge impact they have had on me and on the many aspects of what my life represents.

To my sisters, **Wendy, Susan, Jill, and Tammy**: Thank you for accepting me as your sister, for loving me no matter what, and for always being there for me.

To my brother, **Mike**: Thank you for putting up with all of your sisters and for the important role you have played in my company and in my life. You couldn't be a better brother, and I am proud to be your sister.

To my sister-in-law, **Michelle**: You are a wonderful CFO who has always been like a sister to me, even before you officially joined the family.

To each of my three nieces and my only nephew: You filled the gaping hole in my heart from not having children of my own. You gave me motherhood, and I swell with pride at the many accomplishments and strides you have taken in your lives to become who you are. Thank you for loving me and allowing me to play such a huge role in your lives. My life has been more worthwhile because of you:

Ashley: My goddaughter and niece, your beautiful smile lights my world.

Melanie: Your dad would be so proud that you grew up to become a talented and caring nurse.

Amy: You are a fantastic nurse and a loving niece, and I am so proud of you.

Mandy: My "adopted" niece, you could not be more like family to me, nor could I have loved you more if you were.

Brandt: My brilliant nephew, whatever you choose to do with your life, I know you will have passion for it, and you will do it well. I believe in you.

ACKNOWLEDGMENTS

To **Buddy Allen**: You have always been my rock, my protector, and my partner in business. I would not be who I am today without your guidance.

To **Tripp Perrin**: Without your insistence and encouragement, this book would not have come to be. Thank you for your friendship and fresh insights as we prepare to raise the bar even higher in home health.

To **Chip Hortenstein**: If you hadn't helped me with the initial business plan for Care Advantage, I am not sure I would have ever finished it! Thanks for making sure we always add up.

To **Deb Childs**: Thank you for finding just the right words to bring my story to life.

To **My Soul Mate**: Your love will make my life complete.

Closing Thought:

TODAY IS
WHAT YOU MAKE IT—
MAKE IT A GREAT DAY!

THANK YOU

We appreciate you reading this book.
We would love to hear what you have to say about it.

Write to: Heart Knocks, LLC
10041 Midlothian Turnpike
Midlothian, Virginia 23235

Or visit the web site below

AN INVITATION

To follow the events, happenings, prosperous opportunities, and new
offerings by Heart Knocks, LLC, visit the web site often @

www.heartknocks.net

If you would like to have Debbie Johnston speak to your organization
or if you have an interest in individual mentoring, please contact us
through the web site or call 804.323.9464 ext. 20.